The Art of
Awareness

Other Redleaf Press Books by Deb Curtis and Margie Carter

Reflecting Children's Lives, 2nd Edition: *A Handbook for Planning Child-Centered Curriculum*

Designs for Living and Learning: Transforming Early Childhood Environments

Learning Together with Young Children: A Curriculum Framework for Reflective Teachers

The Visionary Director, 2nd Edition: *A Handbook for Dreaming, Organizing, and Improvising in Your Center*

Training Teachers: A Harvest of Theory and Practice

The Art of Awareness

How Observation Can Transform Your Teaching

Second Edition

DEB CURTIS AND MARGIE CARTER

Redleaf Press®
www.redleafpress.org
800-423-8309

Published by Redleaf Press
10 Yorkton Court
St. Paul, MN 55117
www.redleafpress.org

First edition published 2000. Second edition 2013.
Cover design by Jim Handrigan
Cover photograph by leaf / Veer
Interior design by Erin Kirk New and typeset in Adobe Chapparal Pro
Excerpts and adaptations on pages 13, 41, 92, 108–109, and 168–169 are
    from Learning by Heart: *Teachings to Free the Creative Spirit* by Corita
    Kent and Jan Steward. Copyright © 2008 by Corita Kent and Jan
    Steward. Reprinted with permission of Jan Steward and the Corita Art
    Center, Immaculate Heart Community, Los Angeles.
Printed in the United States of America
19   18   17   16   15   14   13   12   1   2   3   4   5   6   7   8

Library of Congress Cataloging-in-Publication Data
Curtis, Deb.
   The art of awareness : how observation can transform your teaching /
Deb Curtis and Margie Carter.
       p. cm.
   Summary: "Observation study sessions help you discover the many
ways that being observant can enhance your teaching. Updates to this
second edition reflect current issues in early childhood education,
including learning standards, assessment, and technology"
— Provided by publisher.
   Includes bibliographical references.
   ISBN 978-1-60554-086-3 (pbk.)
   1. Observation (Educational method) 2. Early childhood teachers.
3. Early childhood education.   I. Carter, Margie, 1942- II. Title.
LB1027.28.C87 2012
372.21—dc23
                        2012032024

Printed on acid-free paper

For Elizabeth Prescott, who first taught us the joy of observation,

and all the early childhood educators thereafter who have been looking

closely and delighting in children with us.

Contents

Acknowledgments

The ideas, experiences, and examples harvested for this book come from more places than we can remember or acknowledge. We apologize for any unintended omission of citations and extend our appreciation to all the instructors, authors, artists, and illustrators from whose work we have drawn inspiration.

A number of teachers and programs generously offered us their time, photographs, and observation stories for the first edition of this book, published in 2000, when digital photography was in its infancy in early childhood settings. So, while we continue to be grateful for their contributions, moving the book to full color with digital photographs meant we had to replace nearly every story and photo for this 2013 edition. For their contributions to this new edition, we give special thanks to the staff at Crescent Park Child Development Center, in Palo Alto, California, including Stephanie Hill, Jess Guiney, Sheena Wilton, Lindsay Juricich, Jesly Morales, Simone Fussell, Uwimana Middleton, Katja Davis, Michael Burrell, Julia Hill-Wright, and Tierney Falkner. Their exceptional child-centered work inspired Deb to work with them in opening a toddler room, and they generously contributed stories and photos to this book. Lorrie Baird, Samantha Monteith, Julie Thompson, Angela Hoar, Norma Curtis, Dianne Traynor, Nicole Kent, and Lisa Delgarno at Kawartha Child Care Services in Peterborough, Ontario, inspired us as they embraced the use of learning stories as a staff development tool, and they generously contributed samples of their work. Shelly Brandon from London Bridge Child Care Services in London, Ontario, contributed several thoughtful stories about her work with toddlers. Sarah Felstiner, Emily Viehauser, Sandra Floyd, and Jill Loreto of Hilltop Children's Center in Seattle, Washington, continued to offer us terrific examples of how observation can inspire and transform one's teaching practice. After fifteen years of work at Hilltop, Ann Pelo has moved on to other endeavors, but her contributions to this book remain strong. Karina Rojas, Luz Casio, Elida Sangerman, and Laura McAlister offered us lovely observations and photos of their work to begin to practice the art of awareness in their bilingual centers of Sound Child Care Solutions, also in Seattle. For many years we've worked with the consultants and cohort teachers of United Way Bright Beginnings in Houston, Texas, and watched them grow in documenting their offerings of invitations of beautiful materials to children. Shannon McClelland, Kasondra Brown, Sanjuana Frank, Fran Brockington, Dana Hampton, Lorna Patterson, Patricia Hernandez, and Daisy Machac made contributions to this book from their teacher cohort work. Thanks to Betsy Surtshin and Victoria Varela of the Osher Marin JCC Child Development Center in San Rafael, California; Elizabeth Hicks, Christine Borgel, Cheryl Scott, and Cheryl Miller of the Point Pleasant Child Care Centres of Halifax, Nova Scotia; and Darlene Nantarath of the Acorn School in Toronto, Ontario. Yvonne Walker and Megan Montoya in the Phoenix, Arizona, area sent us detailed observations of the competencies of the special needs children with whom they work. Sue Briton of the Paradise Valley Community College Cohort Project in Phoenix made stories and photos available from our work there.

We are deeply appreciative of the inspiring work of our colleagues in Aotearoa, New Zealand, for the way they have taught us about including *whānau* families in documentation and the use of learning stories as both an assessment tool and professional development vehicle. Our study of their remarkable work and ongoing visits to centers have truly enhanced our understandings. Special thanks to Lorraine Manuel, Hanna Fale, and Jen Boyd at Tots Corner; Thelma Chapman at Awhi Whānau Early Childhood Centre; Karen Wiley at Te Puna Kohungahunga; Jenny Jones at Magic Garden Care and Education Centre; Adrienne Wilkins, Maria Riepen, and Emma Parsons at Sophia's Preschool; Chris Bayes and Gemma Smith in the Foundations Class at the Diocesan School for Girls; Wendy Lee at the Educational Leadership Project; and Margaret Carr at the University of Waikato in New Zealand. Gratitude to Peg Callaghan, Nancy Gerber, Donna King, and Kelly Ramsey, colleagues who continue to bring us photos and detailed stories about their time with children.

Thanks to Kerry Ruef and the folks at the Private Eye who first introduced us to—and generously supplied us with—jeweler's loupes. And to Paul Fleishman who inspired us with his poems in two voices.

Our appreciation goes to David Heath, Douglas Schmitz, and the entire team at Redleaf Press who continue to strengthen the coherence and presentation of our work and help us to communicate our message to the early childhood field. They are a pleasure to work with.

And, as always, we are grateful to our families and friends, who continue to believe in and support us even as we get consumed by book projects. Their encouragement to pursue our passion for children and those who care for them makes it possible for us to do this work.

Two Voices within a Teacher

I'm an early childhood teacher

I think of my work as

very demanding   very stimulating

It's as if I'm

an air traffic controller	an architect designing an environment for discovery
trying to keep everyone on course and prevent collisions	a gardener, tilling the soil, planting seeds for a love of learning
a bodyguard	teaching the children how to share and get along with others

The learning environment I create is clean and organized.

I'm always buying new curriculum materials and learning games	I arrange things with discovery and beauty in mind, choosing things from nature and loose parts for play in the classroom

If I could just

get the children to sit still and listen   take time to sit and listen to them

I could

teach them what they need to be ready for school	discover their questions and encourage their curiosity so they'll be excited about learning

I'm worried

they don't learn enough when they just play   they don't get enough time to play

There's so little time

to get everything I've planned done	to experience the wonder of childhood
Children need to be challenged to pay close attention and follow directions	Children must have time to race down the hill, splash through that puddle, sit under a tree, and gaze at the clouds

Watching children play

doesn't make me look like a real teacher

is the part of my job I love most
Children do and say the most remarkable things

It's true, children sometimes surprise me
with what they know

I'm amazed by their insights and abilities

I know it's important to observe

each child has to be assessed for progress

each child has so much to teach me
Watching closely, I see so much growth
unfolding

I so want

the parents to see me as a legitimate teacher

the parents to delight with me in what
their children are doing

I have so much I want to cover with
my curriculum

So much of my curriculum comes from
my observations

When I let the children have free play

I have to have eyes in the back of my head
to keep them safe and out of mischief

I see how they benefit from taking risks,
and how inventive and capable they really are

This work

has so many pressures and demands

is sooo rewarding!

I'm thinking

about looking for another job

this job is one I want to keep for as long
as possible

Introduction

If you're an early childhood teacher, no doubt your head is full of tugging voices and questions: What are the children really learning as they play? How should I handle all this pressure for school readiness? What will reassure parents that I'm a competent teacher? How long can I really stay in this job?

Competing interests in young children's futures storm around and within us. Early childhood teachers feel so much pressure to shape children into what society expects of them. There is an ever-growing body of quality rating scales and professional and state standards that early childhood educators must be accountable for. In quieter moments, we long to be with children in a different way. Then the prevailing tide rushes in with the language of QRIS, early learning frameworks, and accreditation criteria. The wonder of childhood is pulled under and washed away once more, and with it, our love of teaching.

Waiting for you in the eye of this storm are the art of awareness and the joy of paying close attention to children. With close observation, you can refocus, see the value of childhood and children's remarkable competencies, and remember why you wanted to be a teacher. You can learn to integrate the concerns of these contesting voices. A full measure of delight can return to your work with children. If observation is already part of your teaching practice, you may find an expanded focus in this book to deepen your work into a more intellectually engaging and joyful practice. If observation isn't at the center of your practice, developing the art of awareness can transform your teaching, your job satisfaction, and your commitment to a career in the early childhood field.

Refocusing Our Work

The early childhood profession faces a critical juncture. We have come of age as a full-fledged profession with a core body of knowledge, code of ethics, professional standards, accreditation systems, credentials, research, professional literature, and a multitude of conferences for ongoing professional development. These developments are all wonderful. In addition, policy makers and

funders are understanding the importance of early-years education for brain development and later success in school. But for practicing early-years teachers, these developments often translate into giving more attention to rating scales and accountability systems than to the children themselves. This assessment-driven reality reflects the overall trend in education in the United States.

In the United States, there is no clear vision for the value of children or the role of childhood in our collective lives. We are willing to entertain children, make products for them to consume, and prepare children for adulthood. Yet we don't earnestly give them much attention for who they are *right now*. We overlook the insights children offer us. Except for brief moments of crisis, holidays, or campaigning for elections, rarely do the lives of children get public attention. The general public doesn't discuss how children enrich our humanity and our overall culture. Even parents and teachers fail to notice what children notice, and they don't let children lead us to a new awareness and appreciation for their time of life. Professor and author David Elkind reminds us in *The Hurried Child* that in the last fifty years, our country has become more and more adult oriented, with children increasingly viewed as a nuisance. Shopping malls, casinos, health clubs, and the Internet have all been conspicuously developed as places for adults to gather. Parks, neighborhoods, and schools have been neglected. Most early childhood and school-age programs are isolated from the rest of the world. This contributes to this generational apartheid in our communities. Strange as it seems, early childhood workplaces have grown to mirror, rather than transform, the invisibility of children in our society at large.

The early childhood field itself is a clear target of commercial interests. This is ironic, because we are marginalized and devalued in the overall allocation of resources and public attention. We, too, often behave as if we've lost our way. Rather than steadily cultivating a vision for ourselves, we often just follow the latest trend. In our professional meetings and conferences, we are persuaded to spend our time rushing rather than relating, consuming rather than creating. Professional development and meetings rarely focus on children's words, feelings, experiences, or thought processes.

Taking Up the Invitation

Children can awaken in us an understanding of being inventive, engaged, delighted, and determined to rearrange the world. If we listen to and watch them closely, they will teach us to be more observant, inquisitive, and responsive in our work and lives. It isn't easy to pay attention to children in this way. So much conspires to take us in other directions. The daily crush of tasks and pleas for attention is enormous. Our requirements and accountability systems, our schedules and meetings and learning goals can easily push childhood out of the picture. Unlike children, we adults have so many pressing agendas that we often miss what is right under our noses. Children invite us to take a closer look. This book invites you to learn the art and skill of observation. Doing so has the potential to change your life, not just your teaching, for the better.

The late Anita Olds, an expert in designing spaces for early childhood, used to say of licensing requirements, "Children are miracles, not minimums!" They come to us full of wonder, eager to understand and be competent. Yet despite our good intentions to teach them, we adults easily begin to deplete children's innate wellspring of zest for learning. In *An American Childhood*, Annie Dillard puts it this way:

> No child on earth was ever meant to be ordinary, and you can see it in them, and they know it too. But then the times get to them, and they wear out their brains learning what folks expect, and spend their strength trying to rise over those same folks. (Dillard 1993, 208)

When we neglect to see who children really are, we deprive ourselves of deeper sources of delight. We miss the opportunity to witness the profound process of human development that is unfolding before our eyes. Becoming a careful observer of young children reminds us that what might seem ordinary at a superficial glance is actually quite extraordinary. In a class she taught, early childhood author Elizabeth Prescott compared a string of ordinary moments for a child to beads on a necklace, each one unique yet related to the others, combining to create an unfolding work of wonder.

To be sure, some children don't appear as wonderful to us as others. They are the real challenges to our vision. Sometimes these children almost require us to use a magnifying glass to see what is really there. Taking the time for deeper glimpses into the play, work, and thinking of challenging children makes our job one of continual exploration, invention, and flexible thinking. If we can keep our focus, we will get through the rough and bumpy times, past our blind spots, to find some new perspectives on even the most difficult children. One of the goals of this book is to help you develop the ability to notice details and adopt different perspectives. Bringing liveliness and enthusiasm to your work life is another.

Listening, Observing, and Documenting Is a Pedagogy

When we begin to value *who* children are (not just what we want them to be), a shift happens in the way we think about learning and teaching. Our jobs become more engaging and fulfilling. We also begin to envision a larger purpose for our profession. We strive to make childhood visible and valued for the ways that it can enrich our humanity and contribute to our collective identity. To bring this transformation about, we need a pedagogy (a way of thinking about learning and teaching) that mirrors our vision for children. We don't want to promote one that exists in the popular culture. We need to move away from commercially packaged activities. We need to make the time to develop curriculum collaboratively with our coworkers, the children, and their families. We must focus our attention away from the clocks and checklists to see what is going on with the children themselves. Teachers who subscribe to a pedagogy like this come from a place of curiosity. They believe in children's capabilities and know that they are engaging in a process that is not static; it's unfolding.

The benefits of this approach are far-ranging. Moving children into the center of our focus teaches us more about child development. We begin to understand the learning involved in self-chosen play and the components of a curriculum shaped around children's perspectives. Looking closely, we can see the influence of cultural patterns. This helps us learn more about ourselves, our preferences, our biases, and our blind spots. Discussing our observations with coworkers and children's families helps us to see things from different perspectives, allowing each of us to transcend the limitations of our own points of view. We create a collective context for mutual respect and learning from each other.

Gathering observation notes and other forms of documentation and sharing them as stories of children's pursuits gives the children and their stories more visibility, meaning, and respect. The learning process is enhanced for the children as well as the adults. College professor and author George Forman puts it this way:

> We know that making children's ideas visible is an important goal. It helps children convert an activity into a learning encounter. Therefore, if documentation helps children make their own feelings, patterns of behavior, theories, and rules more visible and explicit, then documentation could become the primary means of educating young children. (Online dialogue on Reggio listserv discussion, 1999)

Where can we see this pedagogy in action? Many would point to the schools of Reggio Emilia in Italy and in the schools they have inspired around the world, including Australia, New Zealand, Canada, and the United States. We can see the seeds of this approach in the teaching and writing of Karen Gallas, Elizabeth Jones, Vivian Paley, Gretchen Reynolds, and Carol Anne Wien. Their books are rich with descriptions of children's play and teachers negotiating their roles in it. Teachers can turn to these writers' works again and again for reminders and inspiration about how children's lives can be valued and our differing perspectives on them can be negotiated.

Several practicing early childhood teachers have also written books, giving us a firsthand, vivid picture of how this pedagogy has been developed in their classrooms. Ann Pelo worked as a preschool teacher/author in a full-time child care program. Her teaching is featured in a series of staff training videos: *Children at the Center*, *Setting Sail*, *Thinking Big*, *Building Bridges between Teachers and Families*, *To See Takes Time*, and *Side by Side* (available at www.ecetrainers.com). Pelo describes her evolving pedagogy of listening, observing, and documenting in the book she coauthored with Fran Davidson, *That's Not Fair!* (Pelo and Davidson 2000).

> When I first began the practice of taking notes about children's play and making recordings of children's conversations, I didn't really understand how to use all the documentation I gathered. I did it because I'd read about it being the right thing to do. I'd carefully transcribe a recorded conversation among children, then go on with the plans I'd already made. I mostly thought of the notes and conversations as ways to capture on paper the sweet and appealing thinking of young children. I'd share my transcriptions with parents, inviting them to "listen in" on conversations that they would otherwise miss.
>
> As I grew into the practice of supporting emerging projects, I learned more about how to use the documentation that I collected. I noticed myself wishing to understand if my guesses about the children's interests were on target or way off base, knowing that it mattered deeply to the success of an emerging project. I began to turn to my carefully collected notes for guidance. When I studied my notes and transcriptions alone or with a coteacher, I could see underneath the children's words to the themes and issues undergirding them. I noticed when ideas were repeated or when a theme showed up over and over. I began to see through to the heart of children's play. And with an understanding of the heart of their play, I could respond in meaningful ways and take an active role in shaping an activism project. I could better supply the classroom with props that would sustain play. I could plan trips or invite visitors to the classroom. I could ask provocative questions of the children. I could develop strategies for the children to represent their thinking. Listening to the children is my best guide for supporting emerging projects. The documentation I collect while the children play and talk deepens my listening. (Pelo and Davidson 2000, 76, 78)

Later Pelo went on to author *The Language of Art: Inquiry-Based Studio Practices in Early Childhood Settings* (2007), in which she describes how she used her observations to design in-depth studies for children using art media as "thinking tools." You'll see examples of this kind of work in several of the chapters of *The Art of Awareness*.

First-grade teacher Karen Gallas has written a number of books charting her journey as a teacher. Gallas makes children's words, actions, and artistic expressions a focal point for her own development. In her book *The Languages of Learning*, Gallas (1994, 5–6) describes her pedagogy of creating the classroom as a research community.

This process of data collection is ongoing. It becomes part of the life of the classroom and is absorbed into the interactions between teacher and students. Thus, over the course of a school year, I compile an enormous amount of information that helps me to reflect on the classroom and to answer my more difficult questions about teaching, learning, and the process of education. . . . As a teacher-researcher, I do not determine beforehand the categories of information I am looking for, the nature of the data, or the questions to be asked. Data collection is not a process used only for assessing children's learning or evaluating curricula. The process of data collection, as it has evolved, has become a central part of my classroom practice.

Vivian Gussin Paley is a well-known classroom teacher and author with more than a dozen published books. Her writing reveals the richness of children's perspectives, along with the thinking process of an evolving teacher. In describing how her approach to teaching evolved, Paley says that in her early days of teaching, she found herself having trouble remembering who each of her twenty-six to thirty kindergartners were. At night she would develop schemes to try to remember each of their names, all of which failed. It was only when she set herself the task of writing a few sentences about something each child did or said that she solved this problem and began to know each individual.

This strategy engaged Paley for a while, but as it became routine, she found herself getting bored. Author Margie Carter recalls the following conversation with Vivian Paley from October 1999:

"Bored!" exclaimed a teacher listening to this story. "How could you possibly be bored with twenty-six to thirty children to tend to? You must have been frantically busy!"

"Of course I was extremely busy," Paley replied, "but that's very different than being bored. When I say I was bored, I don't mean with the children, I mean with myself and my job. I didn't find myself very curious, emotionally or intellectually engaged in what was going on. And because I was basically too lazy to go out and look for another job, I decided I had better make this one more interesting. So I began to create little games for myself that forced me to watch more closely what was going on. I'd try doing something one way with the morning group and then a different way with the afternoon class and then asked myself what worked better. I experimented with questions about how boys and girls might respond differently, about what other activities might be least interfered with by the loud noise of carpentry, and so on. And, of course, once I approached my work with this kind of inquiry, everything changed for me. I discovered the remarkable world of children's perspectives and the unending delight of trying to understand the meaning of their play and stories."

Becoming a Keen Observer

What will it take for our early childhood classrooms to be filled with teachers who view children and their work with this mind-set? Ann Pelo, Karen Gallas, and Vivian Gussin Paley offer us valuable models for how teachers can develop themselves by observing children's development. Each of these educators has developed a teaching practice based on her deep respect for children and her curiosity about who they are. The curricula each of them created lead to the very same learning outcomes listed in conventional lesson plans. But they use an emergent planning process with more meaning and relevancy for the children. Throughout this book, you'll find teacher observation stories that provide examples of how observation can transform your teaching.

Becoming a keen listener and observer is certainly the foundation of the art of awareness. If you consult a dictionary, you'll discover that the definition of the word *keen* includes "showing a quick and ardent responsiveness; enthusiastic, eager, intellectually alert, extremely sensitive in perception" (*Merriam-Webster's Collegiate Dictionary*, 11th edition).

But rather than fostering enthusiasm, most instruction on observation turns it into a tedious, arduous process, not the experiences that Pelo, Gallas, and Paley describe. As teachers face increasing requirements to use checklists and complete assessments, observing loses even more vitality. If we as a profession allow this to happen, we will sacrifice one of the most joyful, engaging, and intellectually stimulating experiences teachers can have. Children, in turn, lose the possibility of having their play and ideas taken seriously. Their activities are less likely to be what Forman describes as "learning encounters."

When you see your primary teaching role as closely observing children and communicating what you see, you'll find yourself surrounded by amazing learning encounters. Becoming a keen observer is a way to learn child development, to find curriculum ideas, and to meet requirements for assessing outcomes. It's also a way to keep from burning out in a stressful job. The *Art of Awareness* offers you a series of activities to develop yourself toward that end.

Inspiration from New Zealand

In the years between the first and second editions of this book, 2000 to 2013, we as authors have had the good fortune to meet many fine educators. Among them we have encountered the remarkable commitment of the Ministry of Education in New Zealand and the inspiring work of early childhood educators there. They in turn have drawn inspiration from the international community, influenced by the schools of Reggio Emilia, Italy. The Ministry of Education has crafted a new early childhood system that honors the Treaty of Waitangi, creating an inclusive environment for all New Zealanders and, specifically, the Maori people. We have studied their transformational process. Our annual visits to New Zealand have given us a firsthand picture of their teaching practice. It is based on a view of children as competent and deserving of respect, while valuing different cultural funds of knowledge as equally worthy.

We encountered Margaret Carr, a professor at the University of Waikato, and her important work on using Learning Stories as a tool for assessment and professional development (*Assessment in Early Childhood Settings: Learning Stories*, Sage Publications, 2001) as well as her newest book with Wendy Lee, *Learning Stories: Constructing Learner Identities in Early Education* (2012). Her work has strongly influenced our ongoing teacher-education work. Together with our colleague Tom Drummond and in consultation with Carr and her colleague Wendy Lee, we have adapted the Learning Story approach for a North American audience. We have seen inexperienced and mature teachers alike adopt the Learning Story approach to study their observations. They have written stories based on their observations that reveal new insights into children's perspectives. In addition, they have discovered a stronger sense of their own role in telling the stories of working with children. You will see examples of this throughout this book.

Using This Book

This book begins with a series of study sessions designed to heighten your observation skills. These chapters differ from other texts on observing because they are designed to help you learn to *really see* children. This observation is not for the purpose of analyzing or doing anything to or for them, but simply to value who they are and the experience of childhood. The study sessions include activities to help you replace what you hope to see and any labels or preconceptions you might have with a simple appreciation of the descriptive details of what you are actually seeing. This is important because we all observe subjectively through the filters of our own experiences and values.

The first four study sessions offer foundational ideas and practical strategies to expand your self-awareness. The more aware you become of the things that influence your ability to hear and see, the closer you get to objectivity. Chapter 2 is a study session on learning to see; chapter 3 is a study session on observing for children's perspectives; chapter 4 is a study session on observing children's lively minds; and chapter 5 is a study session on observing how children use their senses.

These sessions are followed by six chapters that you study on specific aspects of childhood. Again, you will be asked to let go of your adult agenda or your teacher urge to do something with what you are seeing. Instead, you will replace this with the goal of really seeing what's there. In the Buddhist tradition, this is referred to as *mindfulness*.

Following these study sessions, the remaining three chapters of the book offer you ideas and strategies for getting organized to observe, for using and sharing your observations, and for using your observations for planning and assessment.

Photographs and observation stories, often with transcriptions of children's conversations, are used throughout all the chapters of *The Art of Awareness*. These are as valuable for you to study as the text itself. You will also find examples of teachers' self-reflections and communications with the children's families to model how observations can be used and displayed.

Choosing How to Live and Work

Our world is fraught with so many challenges that many of us try to survive by numbing ourselves, thus losing our attentiveness. *The Art of Awareness* offers an antidote to that narrowing, if not debilitating, choice for how to be in the world. Living in the details of the human spirit leads to more mindfulness, liveliness, and overall pleasure in your life. If you take the time to notice, each child offers a glimpse of something promising in the world. When you make what you value and notice more visible to yourself and to others, it becomes a resource for change. Together we can create an active vision for becoming individuals and a collective culture that holds children and childhood as sacred and worthy of our utmost attention.

Chapter 1

A New Way of Being with Children:
An Overview of the Study Sessions

It takes practice for us to recover this ability to see, or before that, the gift of wanting to see. For so many years we have been learning to judge and dismiss—I know what that thing is, I've seen it a hundred times— and we've lost the complex realities, laws, and details that surround us. Try looking the way the child looks—as if always for the first time.
—CORITA KENT AND JAN STEWARD

As you read the following story about Karina's classroom, consider the role that observation plays in her teaching. How does her close attention to the children's knowledge and interests influence what happens in her classroom?

As Karina sets up the room for her day with children, she decides to offer buttons in a new way. She takes them off the shelf and places them on one of the tables as an invitation for the children to discover. She puts the buttons in a basket and lays out some pieces of construction paper with different shapes glued on them. Karina is in the early stages of shifting her teaching away from the practice of making all table activities teacher-directed lessons. She's very curious about what the children will do when they discover these materials she's placed on the table.

The first few children who approach the table seem hesitant. They ask Karina what they are supposed to do. She smiles and says, "You are welcome to play with the buttons. See what you can discover." As these girls sit down, several others join them and the fun begins. The children are clearly sifting through the buttons, describing what they are discovering and finding different ways to set them on the paper. Karina stays close by, noticing how the children are investigating the buttons and periodically describing what she sees them doing. She does her best to avoid asking questions such as "What color is that?" or "How many buttons do you have?" It's new for her to just take a few notes and photos of things the children are doing and saying. She's eager to learn more about their interests and the experiences that come out during their play.

The first thing that strikes Karina is the variety of ways children explore the buttons. Some seem quite focused and serious. Others are exuberantly grabbing, relishing the abundance of buttons. Some children have begun sorting and classifying the buttons by color, size, or shape. One child starts a treasure hunt, trying to find all the big buttons with "gold petals on the outside." Another child picks up random buttons one at a time and then methodically places them on her paper. One of the quieter solo workers at the table creates what is clearly the representation of a person.

After putting buttons on his paper, one child discovers that if he blows on a button, it will scoot across the table. He is thrilled with his discovery, calling out, "Look! Look what I did! Look what I did! It's flying. Flying up. That one jumped." Karina comes over for a closer look. "Wow, you really made a discovery. You can use your breath to move the air so it will move the buttons." Before long, others join him in this activity. They invent a button-blowing game, making up rules as they go along. Karina is amazed that the children have used the buttons in ways that never would have occurred to her. At one point, she turns her camera around and shows one of the children a series of pictures she has captured. It is the progression of ideas the child has had over the last twenty minutes. The girl is eager to describe what she was doing in every photo.

Karina realizes she is puzzled by something. She notices that none of the children seem to make use of the shapes on the paper for their button work. In fact, several children have turned the paper over so the blank side is facing up. She wonders what this means about their exploration of space and lines. She can't wait to talk with her assistant teacher about all her observations so they can consider how they might offer the buttons next time.

This small glimpse of Karina's work with children is rich with the elements of the teaching approach presented in this book. Working with children in this way is quite different from focusing on cookie-cutter curriculum activities. It also goes beyond traditional observation practices, in which teachers collect data primarily for the purpose of assessment and measuring outcomes. While this is a valid reason for observing, it is more limited than what we as authors are suggesting in this book. In fact, what you see in Karina is a teacher engaged in ongoing professional development. She is practicing close observation, flexible thinking, risk taking, and working without a known outcome. She demonstrates the ability to move in and out of analysis while staying in the present moment. This ability helps her use the children's exploration as a source of planning, not to mention inspiration.

When approaching observation in this open-ended way, teachers must view children as competent creators of their own understandings. They see children as individuals who deserve the time and attention needed for their experiences to unfold with deeper meaning. Teachers like Karina see the richness of these childhood moments and value children's perspectives and pursuits. Teachers who use this approach spend their time observing children, working to uncover their point of view and understandings. They do not spend time planning lessons and filling out developmental checklists. They use their observations to guide their responses and ongoing planning. They then draw on them for filling out developmental data or school-readiness assessments.

Reread the story, study the photos, and notice the specific things Karina is doing in her teaching practice.

- Karina provides open-ended materials for the children to explore. She understands the kinds of materials that engage children. She chooses materials with texture, beauty, complexity, and a range of possibilities for use.

- She offers materials with attention to order and aesthetics, which will call forth the children's interest and help them focus on the possibilities.

- Karina observes closely and documents the details of ordinary moments of the children's explorations and actions. She sometimes spontaneously shares her observations with the children by describing what she is seeing and showing them photos of their work.

- Karina shares her delight in what the children are doing. She asks open-ended questions and avoids questions that seek a particular answer, but rather keeps a curious, open mind, wondering why the children are pursuing particular activities.

- Even when a child uses the buttons in an unexpected way, such as blowing them, Karina admires his ingenuity. She does not offer a rule.

- Karina is eager to share her observations with other teachers to see if their perspectives can suggest additional ideas about what is occurring and what might be offered next.

Why Study Sessions?

Because of the many demands and distractions teachers face, learning to pay close attention to children requires systematic study and ongoing practice. This book offers you that opportunity. The study sessions were originally designed as a college course to counter the notion that observing children is a cumbersome task. The sessions offer you an organized system that will help you become aware of children in a new way. Through practice, you will discover that developing the art of awareness is one of the most stimulating and nourishing things you can do for yourself and for children. It will make your job easier and more enjoyable.

You will find that these study sessions are not designed as checklists to use or facts to learn. Rather, they offer new ideas, activities, and experiences to help you invent a different way of *being* with children. Each session will take you through a set of activities designed to help you slow down, become self-aware, and pay attention. You will develop your ability to think flexibly, critically, and in depth. Teachers who have participated in these sessions have found them useful for their work with children and even in other parts of their lives. Here are some of their comments as they've undertaken the study sessions:

Today I watched a toddler walk by my house holding his grandmother's hand. I watched from my window as he took tiny steps and stopped a number of times to step on a leaf, kick the grass, and point out some berries that had fallen on the ground. Since taking this class, I now wonder what it's like to be entertained by stepping on leaves and grass and pointing to bright objects that I notice. I realize how much I pass by things and do not even notice them. I am quick to judge things that I've seen before. Now I have become more curious about things, and I am learning more and noticing more about the little things around me. It is so refreshing.
—LINDSEY

I feel myself being stretched and growing. As I observe children playing now, I find myself examining their play in greater detail. I realize how I never really watched them before. I feel bad about it, but now I know so much more is going on than I thought.
—JUDI

I feel challenged, but also I'm really going through a learning process. I see now that observing is a process. The quotes have really made me think. The art of awareness activities give me a different perspective. And the observation practice has helped me become really skilled at noticing details. I see the world around me so differently than I did a few months ago. I see it clearer and with more delight. It's a new beginning!
—GAIL

This class has taught me a new way to observe not only children but everything. It is different from anything I have ever taken. I never had to look at things before. I'm still trying to figure it out. It's hard sometimes, but I'm learning so much.
—BECKY

Components of the Study Sessions

The first four study sessions—chapters 2, 3, 4, and 5—provide foundational skills that will help you begin paying close attention to the children you work with. The next seven study sessions—chapters 6 through 11—are all organized similarly. Each of these focuses on observing a particular aspect of childhood. Each study session ends with an example of a teacher's observation story that was formally written up and posted in the program or on a blog or other online platform.

Chapter 2, the first study session, is "Learning to See." In it, you will learn to examine how your own experiences influence your perceptions. There will be opportunities to practice noticing the difference between your interpretations and the details of what you are looking at.

Chapter 3 is "Observing for Children's Perspectives" and offers strategies on how to shift from your teacher agenda toward finding children's points of view and the importance of their life in the here and now. This session will be the beginning of a number of activities calling you back to your own favorite childhood experiences to help you put yourself in children's shoes more easily. As you make the shift to seeing children's actions from their perspective, you will be reminded of how capable they really are. This view of children and the respect and trust it generates will transform your teaching.

Chapter 4 introduces you to "Observing Children's Lively Minds." You will be introduced to examples of how close observation can reveal that even the very youngest children can focus intently, investigate materials, and communicate an eagerness to learn more.

Chapter 5, "Observing How Children Use Their Senses," provides examples of how children use all of their senses to explore new things they encounter.

The study sessions in chapters 2 to 11 are all organized in the same way to help you practice skills and revisit the focus of each chapter through a variety of activities. The consistent structure of the sessions will help you develop both left- and right-brain skills. The left-brain skills help you notice the details of children's experiences. The right-brain skills involve the awareness associated with artists or naturalists. Detailed observation stories of children are included in each chapter, highlighting the aspect of childhood focused on in that chapter.

As you go through each study session, you will find the following components:

Quotation about Seeing

We walk around believing that what we see with our eyes is real, when, in truth, each of us constructs our own understandings of what we are seeing.
—DONALD HOFFMAN

To remind you that everyone sees things differently, each of the study sessions begins with a quote and then a reflection like the one you just read by Donald Hoffman. These quotes come from artists, naturalists, poets, and others who spend time carefully reflecting on what they see. Use these quotes to spark, provoke, or challenge you to see how your own experiences may affect how you see the world, children, and yourself as a teacher.

In *Visual Intelligence: How We Create What We See,* Donald D. Hoffman (2000) tells the story of a man who regained his sight after being blind from infancy. Hoffman describes the great difficulty this man had in making sense of what he saw. Nothing was recognizable, and everything was confusing, because he had no experience with the world of sight. He needed to shut his eyes to function because all of his understandings came through his other senses. This story is a powerful illustration of how we each see the world through our own experiences, biases, and filters. Having this awareness in our work with children helps us observe with more self-understanding and thoughtfulness.

Learning Goals for This Study Session

This list provides an overview of the learning goals for the study session you are about to undertake. You can refer back to this list as you move through or complete the study session. The list can help you reflect on what you learned and help you identify what you may have missed.

Reflect on the Quote

In this section, you will be asked questions to help you to reflect on a quote such as Hoffman's quote about seeing. Then you will have the opportunity to write about your reactions and thoughts and about the implications they have for your work with children. You are encouraged to share your responses and ideas with others. You also might want to gather a collection of these quotes, post them, or keep them with you to help you stay alert to the limits of your own perspectives. They can inspire you to see more.

Art of Awareness Activities

To give children and childhood the attention they deserve, we must bring a different mind-set to our work. As Corita Kent and Jan Steward suggest in the quote that begins this chapter, we need to recover our ability to see, rather than judge and dismiss. The art of awareness activities in each study session will challenge your immediate responses and judgments. They are designed to help you move beyond first impressions and quick labels. Many of the activities are not directly related to children but come instead from the work of artists, psychologists, and naturalists.

The learning activities offered here do not follow a traditional approach to teacher education. They are intended to sharpen the overall awareness you bring to your work with children. Some of the activities will help you practice flexible thinking and shift your perspective. Others will ask you to tap your own creativity and express unique ideas. Don't be surprised if you find your head spinning or if you feel unbalanced. Becoming unsettled is part of a learning process that will give you more awareness as a teacher.

If you approach the art of awareness activities in earnest, they will help you reclaim your own sense of wonder and curiosity. Children approach the world with clear eyes and a refreshing perspective. They always raise their heads to marvel at an airplane when they hear its engines roar. They let ice cream linger on their tongues and drip down their chins. They stop to investigate the cracks in the sidewalk.

Learning the art of awareness will help you approach the world as children do, with openness and the use of all of your senses. Your life and work will be richer for it.

Remembering Your Childhood

Each study session is organized around a particular childhood theme. These are themes teachers see every day in their work. To learn more about the significance of the childhood theme, you will be asked to recall the details and feelings of your own experiences. Your own experiences will set the stage for the observation stories that follow.

Sample Observation and Observation Practice

Samples of observation stories are included in each session. Use them to study the details that hold the meaning and significance of the experience for the children. As you study the details in each story, you will learn how to collect and describe similar details while you observe. These stories offer you a snapshot of ordinary moments of childhood. Consider them invitations to be treasured and rich information to help you learn more about children. Some stories are followed by further reflections from the teachers who captured those observations as they studied the story again.

Following each observation practice, you will be offered some questions. Use them to help you look more closely at the details of the story. Try to discover the meaning and significance of these details for the children. This will give you practice in looking deeper, beyond your own filters and teaching agendas. You can do this reflection on your own or with others.

Take Another Look

After studying the observation stories, you will be invited to apply the ideas to your own setting. The questions and activities will enhance your own practice and study about this particular aspect of childhood. You will find areas to examine, materials or activities to add to your environment, and suggestions for additional focused observations. As you continue to practice using these ideas and skills with children, they will become second nature to you. You will begin to readily value children's pursuits and become more creative in providing for them.

More Things to Do

Each study session offers additional ideas for more self-awareness and development activities. These will help you learn more about yourself, develop your awareness, and adjust your attitudes toward children.

Sample Observation Display

The study sessions end with an example of a fully developed written observation that a teacher has chosen to develop into a display with photos. As you study these, ask yourself what in the story might have influenced the teacher to take the time to share it in this way. Whether you post your stories online or print them up for a display in your program, the decision to take the time to do so should be guided by how you want others to see children, your values, and the children's particular perspectives and competencies.

How to Use the Observation Study Sessions

The guidelines in each of the study sessions suggest ways you can work on your own, with a partner, or as part of a group. Whenever possible, find another person to work with. This collaborative study can be arranged in any number of settings, depending on your use of this book. They could be used in staff meetings, college classes, seminars, mentoring programs, informally among colleagues, or even with the children's families. Working with others will give you a variety of perspectives, more lively discussions, and more in-depth understandings of the usefulness of the activities in each session. You will always find more details, insights, and possibilities when there are more eyes, ears, and points of view focused on an observation.

The time frame for each session can be adjusted, depending on your individual or group needs and schedule. The activities can easily take a few hours, with additional time devoted to follow-up suggestions. You will need to find a system that works for you, one that helps you discipline yourself for the practice required.

Using and Sharing Your Observations

Chapter 12 moves away from the study session format and offers ideas for getting yourself organized to observe and gather documentation. We offer an extensive set of questions you can use to study. You can also use them to help you make meaning of your observations as you uncover the story you feel is most significant to share with others. Chapter 13 reminds you that while documentation is often seen as a display or a formal product, the documentation process affords you a wide range of opportunities for using your observations. For example, you could use them

- as a study tool for your own learning about children and child development
- as a way to explore ideas with the children themselves
- as a source of ideas for enriching your environment and curriculum
- as a way to invite a dialogue with your colleagues and the children's families

Slow Down and Study

You are now ready to start your journey into *The Art of Awareness*. Give yourself time and practice mindfulness. Enjoy what you discover! At times, you may find yourself unsettled because your brain and body have been set in their ways for so long. Perhaps your approach to observing and teaching up to this point has been focused on your adult agenda rather than on seeking to understand and learn from the children's perspectives. You may be a teacher who continually gathers observations and photos of children but not for the purpose of your own study and professional development. Wherever you are in your own journey of practicing the art of awareness, we offer this book as an opportunity to expand the vision you have for yourself and the children in your life.

Chapter 2

Study Session: Learning to See

We do not really see through our eyes or hear through our ears, but through our beliefs. To put our beliefs on hold is to cease to exist as ourselves for a moment.

—LISA DELPIT

Learning Goals for This Study Session

In this study session, you will

- reflect on your own mental filters and how they influence your perceptions
- distinguish the difference between descriptions and interpretations
- recognize the components of observation skills
- practice seeing the details of an observation
- explore flexible thinking with perception exercises

Reflect on the Quote

When learning to observe, we have to begin by examining our own experiences and perspectives. Reread the Lisa Delpit quote above, and think about these questions:

1   What does "seeing through our beliefs" mean to you?

2   What experiences does it remind you of?

3   How do you think this idea relates to your work with children?

You can reflect on this on your own or discuss it with a partner or small group. You might want to use the responses below from other teachers to spark or extend your thinking.

I think this quote means we all like to be right and in control and that it is really hard to let go of our way of seeing and doing things. Sometimes my coteacher and I really disagree about the different ways we handle children's conflicts. When we try to talk about it, we are very defensive. I think we have to find a way to talk together with the understanding that we all have our own point of view and experience. We shouldn't start out thinking one of us is right and one is wrong. We need to find ways to have more open conversations.

—JILL, TODDLER TEACHER

It makes me see why people find it so hard to see another person's point of view. The quote implies we have to let go of not only our ideas but also our identity and who we are. I think people probably find that really scary. Wow! It means to me that we have a lot of work to do to understand each other and ourselves.
—DEE, PRESCHOOL TEACHER

Art of Awareness Activity

Practice Exploring the Influences on Your Perceptions

Before you can observe children with a new set of eyes, you have to recognize your own filters. What influences the way you see things? This is the first step in developing the utmost sensitivity in your perception. The following activity will help you explore examples of these differences in perception. It requires that you work with at least one other person to compare your responses. A group of people will offer you a livelier discussion and more differences to reflect on.

1   Find an interesting photo in a book, magazine, or online that shows a group of people involved in an activity or interaction together. Make enough copies for each person doing this activity.

2   If you are working with a partner, each person should look over the photo for a few minutes. Without talking or writing, make some mental notes about what you see. Notice your emotional reactions to the photo as well as the details of what you see. Next, put the photo away and take turns describing to each other what you saw in the photograph. Each person should describe what you saw without comments or discussion from the other person.

3   If you are working with a group, ask two or three people to volunteer to leave the room. (Volunteers should not be concerned that there will be tricks or judging of people.) Then ask the volunteers to come back into the room one at a time. Give each volunteer a copy of the photo to look over for a minute or two. Ask the volunteer to mentally note the details as well as emotional reactions to the photo. Take the picture away and ask for a verbal description of what the volunteer observed.

4   After everyone has shared what they remember, discuss the differences between their recollections. Use the following questions to guide the discussion.

•   What were the differences in what each person noticed about the photo?

- Why do you think each of you reacted in this way?
- What from your background, experiences, or values may have influenced what you saw in the photo?

Understanding Influences on Perception

Each of us walks around in the world making meaning of what we see, hear, and experience. We have an amazing capacity to take in information and instantly make sense of it. When we can't make sense of something, we feel uncomfortable and out of balance. When we feel this way, we work hard to find an explanation. We want to get back to our normal, comfortable way of seeing the world.

From infancy we have learned how to make sense of what happens around us. We've discovered that facial expressions and body language give us reams of information about a situation. The tone of someone's voice creates a further impression. These are some of the strongest influences on how we see the world today. We instantly size up a situation without even realizing what factors are influencing us. And each of us does this in a different way, with the different filters of our childhood, temperament, and experiences.

If we become more aware of our interpretations, we can analyze the influences that come into play. Past experiences contribute a big part to how we make sense of things. We scan a scene to find what we recognize as familiar and then assign meaning from our past experiences. Our expectations about what we'll see also are part of the process. Consciously or not, we often see exactly what we expect to see. How we feel in the moment strongly influences what we see. If we are tired or cold or just had a disagreement with a friend, these experiences color our perceptions. And, as Lisa Delpit so clearly says in the quote that begins this study session, our values and beliefs rush in as we interpret and judge a situation.

This photo activity offers a reminder of the differences we each bring in making sense of any situation. Some people describe the concrete physical aspects of a scene, while others notice the relationships between the people and objects in the scene. Some people describe the details, while others describe the feelings they get from the photo.

The notion that we all see things differently is obvious. Yet, as we go about our lives, we usually assume that what we see is true and that others must be seeing the same truths we do. When differing views are acknowledged, there is often conflict. We assume that if one of us is right, then the other must be wrong. Many of us are uncomfortable with conflict and try to avoid it. Nevertheless, we can recognize the opportunity that hearing different experiences and new points of view gives us, even if we are uncomfortable. It is an opportunity to expand our thinking and our humanity.

This book challenges you to develop an active, conscious approach to reflecting on and interpreting your observations of children. The task at hand is to keep alert and self-reflective when looking at your own reactions to events and situations. Try to uncover the possible influences on your perceptions. Remind yourself that others are likely to have different, yet valid, points of view. Once you understand that you bring a set of mental filters to any observation, you can use this awareness to examine what you are seeing more carefully. The habit of immediately interpreting what you see limits your vision. You forget that what you are seeing is your own point of view, rather than something outside of yourself. Changing this habit takes ongoing practice and self-reflection, because it is so easy to stay in your own comfort zone.

Another compelling reason to slow down and observe more conscientiously is to make sure you are seeing children in the most competent light possible. The larger educational and political discourse in the United States emphasizes getting children ready for school and remediating their deficits. This limited view of children seeps into our language and practices with children. As the educators of Reggio Emilia remind us, our image of the child affects everything we do. In turn, that limits or enhances the child's potential. When we see children as needy or lacking in some quality or skill, we may limit what we offer them, or we may stop them from pursuing valuable experiences. Using detailed observations that reflect children's competence helps teachers respond to them in ways that call forth their potential.

Observation Practice

The following activities are designed to help you practice seeing with more intentionality. As you participate, try to let go of your preconceptions, which cloud what you see. Don't think about writing or using the observations in any way. Strip away all of the noise inside your head about a right way to do this. Allow yourself to be in the moment for what you can learn.

Practice Noticing Descriptions and Interpretations

One of the most difficult aspects of learning to observe is recognizing the difference between descriptions and interpretations. Use this activity to help you develop your skills in separating descriptive data from interpretation.

Look at the following photos on your own, in a small group, or with a partner. Record all of your responses to the question: What do you see in the photos? Be as specific as possible.

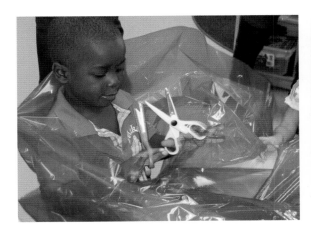 

Practice Creating a Parking Lot

When we observe children, we often have initial responses based on our own mental filters and values. These can get in the way of really seeing the importance of what children are doing. It is helpful to acknowledge these first reactions and then set them aside in a parking lot. You can write these on a separate page of your observation notes. A sample parking lot for a teacher watching this child in the photos above might have notes like this:

- The boy is using the scissors in the wrong way.
- He is goofing around with scissors, trying to get my attention. He should know better than that.
- The scissors are too close to his eyes. I'd better intervene because he's going to hurt himself.

Your first reactions may have merit, and safety issues may require you to jump in quickly to intervene. But unless there is immediate danger, it is important to notice those first reactions and wait before you get involved. When you watch closely, momentarily letting go of your first reactions, you can be more thoughtful about whether to intervene, and if so, how.

Looking over your observation notes from the photo above, decide if anything should be moved to a parking lot away from your descriptive observation data.

Review your notes and compare them to the list below. Notice that the notes are listed in two columns, one labeled *Descriptions* and the other *Interpretations*. When learning to write observation notes, drawing a line down the middle of your paper and using these two categories keeps you mindful of when you are describing and when you are interpreting.

In your work with children, the ultimate goal of observing is to determine the meaning of what is unfolding and to interpret what you see children doing in the most competent light so you can respond in useful ways. In that process, it is important to be aware of the differences between the details and descriptions you gather and your interpretations of the events.

Descriptions	Interpretations
In one photo, the boy is holding two pairs of scissors, one in each hand, with thumb and fingers through the holes.	
He is extending his hands and fingers while he holds the scissors as if to open and close them.	He is interested in examining the scissors to understand how they work.
He is looking closely at the two pairs of scissors he is holding.	He is skillfully comparing the scissors to see how they work together.
In the other photo, the boy has two pairs of scissors; one pair is at rest on the table, and the other pair he is pressing into his cheek. He is smiling.	He is enjoying himself and feeling pleased with what he is doing.

On a new sheet of paper, draw a line down the middle and label the left side *Descriptions* and the right side *Interpretations*. Then use the chart to sort your observation notes from the photo observation activity. Which ones have the details of what actually happened? Which ones have your interpretation of what might have been going on? Don't worry about keeping the sentences together. You may find that the first half of a sentence was an observation and the second half was a reflection. That's okay.

Recognize the Components of Observation Skills

To discover the meaning of an observation, you need descriptive details to support your interpretations. Detailed information helps you discover possible interpretations and misinterpretations from your own filters and biases. The more details, information, and points of view that you uncover, the more options you can generate for responding to the children.

You can learn to observe the details. You must notice when you are interpreting and look closely for the smaller parts that make up the whole. When you find yourself interpreting, stop and ask, "What do I specifically see that leads me to this interpretation?" For example, while observing the child with scissors in the photos, your notes may say, "He is being naughty to get our attention." Or "I'm worried he might hurt himself." What do you specifically see that leads you to these interpretations of his motivations or skills? What in his actions, facial expressions, body language, or tone of voice are you interpreting as naughty or unsafe?

Using these observation skills when we watch children reminds us to look conscientiously for the details of what we are seeing. The details also help us see their competence. They help us to support children's initiative and development of confidence. Below is a list of the components of observing, along with a definition of each, and finally an example of how to apply them in studying the photos of the boy with scissors.

Objectivity: Observe without judging. It is very difficult to be objective, because even if you attempt to suspend your judgment, you are still choosing what to notice when you observe. The best way to be objective is to look for the details then notice your own subjectivity. This can help you put on hold your worry about the safety of the boy with scissors. It allows you to see the details of his competence and the value of his point of view. You may move in closer to him to respond quickly if need be, but try for an instant to see the details that may lead you to more useful perspectives.

The boy is holding two pairs of scissors while looking closely at them as he moves them with his hands and fingers.

Specificity: Look for specific details, such as the number of children and adults involved, the kinds and amount of materials, and the time span of an activity.

It's free choice time in the classroom, and the boy has chosen to work with the scissors and the bright-colored cellophane paper on the table.

Directness: Record direct quotes as much as possible. Still photos obviously don't offer sound, but observers can hear and record what children say.

The boy is smiling as he calls out to those around him, "I can do two at one time."

Mood: Describe the social and emotional details of a situation. These include voice intonation, body language, facial expressions, hand gestures, and other nonverbal information. Mood clues can be difficult to decipher, because we have an automatic, unconscious response to them. We have learned to read mood clues from infancy, and our memories of those early years don't have language associated with them. It takes considerable practice to learn to use mood cues for descriptive details rather than interpretations.

The boy has a focused look on his face as he examines the scissors. He watches his hands as he skillfully opens and closes the scissors. With excitement in his voice, he calls out, "I can do two together."

Completeness: Describe incidents as having a beginning, middle, and end. A complete recording describes the setting, who was involved, the actions in the order they occurred, the responses, interactions, and the ending.

Joshua sat at the table at the beginning of playtime. He began to explore the paper in various ways. He touched it, tried to tear it with his fingers, and tried to cut the paper with the scissors. His attention shifted to the scissors. He put his fingers through both pairs of the scissors and began to open and close them, examining his actions as he worked. After several minutes of trying this action with scissors, he called out, "I can do two together."

Saying, "Joshua is working with scissors" is not a story worth telling. In fact, if you look on the surface, you may stop Joshua's exploration on behalf of using the scissors safely and in the correct manner. If you did this, you would miss the depth and importance of this experience for him. When you notice the details, you are able to marvel at this remarkable childhood moment of exploration and discovery. You can support Joshua's disposition to be a self-directed learner rather than repeatedly correcting his behavior. Using observation skills to assemble the details of the story reveals the richness of the activity. As more and more details come to light, you will notice that these seemingly ordinary, and sometimes challenging, childhood moments offer important opportunities for children to learn about themselves and the world they live in.

Practice Describing the Details

You can also practice noticing details in experiences unrelated to children. This activity can serve as a self-assessment of your skills in describing details. For this activity, you will need another person and two identical sets of small building blocks or toys.

1. Sit back-to-back with a partner. Each of you should have one of the sets of blocks or toys.

2. Build a structure or arrange a design with your blocks.

3. Describe to your partner the building or design you have made. Your partner must try to duplicate the building or design by listening to your directions without looking at what you have done. Neither of you should ask questions.

4. When your partner has finished, look at the outcome together. Discuss what worked and what didn't work about the directions that were given.

5. Switch roles and have the other person take the lead. Follow the same procedures, but see if what you have learned from the first round can help you in this round.

6. When you are finished, consider the differences between the two rounds of building.

After you have completed the activity, discuss the following questions with your partner:

- What happened in the first round when the person described what to build? What did you each discover?

- What success did you have? What did each of you do that helped you succeed?

- What hindered your ability to accomplish this task?

- What else would have helped?

- Did you discover that this was a difficult or an easy task for you?

The task is meant to help you learn the importance of sharing similar understandings and agreed-upon meanings when communicating. The more specific the descriptive details you used, the more likely you were to communicate the directions successfully. You probably found that your interpretations, especially without interaction and feedback, led to misunderstandings. When you collect observations and discuss the details together, you have a better chance of understanding the complexity of what you're seeing. This is more effective than operating from individual opinions and interpretations.

Take Another Look

Once you become aware of the influences on what you see and how easy or hard it is for you to notice and describe details, you are on the road to improving your observation skills. The activity of sitting back-to-back and trying to build what is being described also helps you assess your listening skills. Your ability to hear and see clearly will improve with each step you take to identify what shapes your perceptions. Notice how mood cues may affect your ability to be objective. Identify what you need to overcome as well as what you need to sharpen. Here are some further activities to move you along in this process.

More Exploration of Mental Filters and Their Influences on Perception

Go to a public place like a street corner, park, or mall with a friend or colleague and sit on a bench together to people-watch. Talk together about what you see, challenging each other to give specific details rather than make interpretations. Discuss the differences in what you notice as well as how and why you interpret what you see the same or differently. Write a reflection paper on what you discover.

More Observation Practice—Putting It All Together

Try this activity, either alone or with a partner or small group, to get more practice collecting details, describing what you see, and interpreting your observations.

1 Gather more photos. There are a number of beautiful photography books that can be excellent resources of photos of children with lots of action and emotions portrayed. *The Family of Children* by Jerry Mason (1977) and *From My Side: Being a Child* by Sylvia Chard and Yvonne Kogan (2009) are great resources. You can also go online and search for photos of children to use for your practice. Photos are an easier starting place for practice than live-action videos.

2 To help you make the distinction between descriptions and interpretations, put a line down the center of some paper, labeling one side *Descriptions* and the other *Interpretations*. You might also want to make a separate area for your parking lot to jot down your quick reactions and labels.

3 Write down what you see in the pictures and put your words and phrases under the appropriate category.

4 Review the Components of Observation Skills (pages 30–31) to practice describing more details from your photos.

The more you practice these skills, the better you will become at observing. Once you have ample practice with photos, follow the same process with short video clips of children. Finally, practice with children in real life. Remember to take your time to really see children. Don't worry about a right answer or perfect writing skills.

More to Do

You've completed the first observation study session! You probably will agree that developing this approach and the required skills will take time and practice. Some of your practice should focus on activities that will strengthen your ability to change perspectives. Try to let go of your filters, leave your comfort zone, and accept the insecurity that comes in letting go of your usual ways of looking at things. Included here are a few art-of-awareness activities to try. These activities are not directly related to observing children, but rather are fun experiments that can help you develop flexible thinking—which, of course, has everything to do with your work with children.

Optical Illusions

Which of the horizontal lines in the image below are parallel? How do you know?

Do you see an old or a young woman in this picture? Both images are present if you look closely. With effort, you can switch back and forth from one image to another. Notice the slightly off-balance feeling that happens as you make the switch. Practice switching rapidly back and forth between each of the two images until you can do it comfortably.

Isometric Perspective Designs

Spend some time using colored pencils or markers to color in this design. Notice the changes in perspective you have to make as you work. Study your completed work to continue to practice shifting your perspective.

Source: *Isometric Perspective Designs and How to Create Them* by John Locke (New York: Dover Publications, Inc., 1981). Used by permission.

Magic Eye 3-D Designs

Locate some Magic Eye postcards, calendar pictures, or books, such as *Magic Eye: A New Way of Looking at the World* (by N.E. Thing Enterprises). You can also check out a Magic Eye website at www.magiceye.com. Put the design right up to your nose and very, very slowly pull it away from your face. Look through the image without focusing on it. Try not to blink, and you will discover a hidden image that will magically appear. The key here is to let go of the expectation of seeing something. Only when you do this and really look into the design will an image appear. This is a tricky but useful activity in letting go of expectations and seeing what actually appears.

Spot the Difference/Find the Details

The ability to see details and distinctions does not come easily, nor without practice. A fun way to develop these skills is through the use of spot-the-difference children's books. You can do them alone or with a partner. There are many of these books available in libraries and bookstores. Here is a list of a few favorites:

- *I SPY* from Scholastic Books. There are several of these books available. They challenge you to find specific objects among myriad objects based on a theme or a riddle.

- *Look! The Ultimate Spot-the-Difference Book* by A. J. Wood. At first glance the lush pictures on facing pages seem identical; but take a closer look and discover fascinating differences.

- *Metamorphosis: The Ultimate Spot-the-Difference Book* by Mike Wilks. This is a much more complex spot-the-difference book. It has illustrations and text to compare on facing pages. Adding to its complexity, the underlying theme throughout the book is the cycle of life.

Visual Perception Games

Another way to heighten your ability to notice details is to play games designed around visual perception. These can be played in a group or turned into a game of solitaire. Two great examples are the card game Set™, designed and distributed by Set Enterprises, Inc., www.setgame.com, and the board game Blokus®, designed by Mattel.

Web-Based Perspective Activities

You can find many activities online to practice shifting your perspective. Go online and search for the words *perspective puzzles* and *optical illusions,* or go to YouTube and search for *optical illusions,* and you'll never run out of interesting things to try.

Reflect on Shifting Perspectives

After using any of the resources provided here, do some reflective writing about what you discovered. Here are some examples of teacher reflections.

> At first try, most of these activities make me feel dizzy and give me a headache. But once I work with them, I can feel my brain getting settled, and I am able to have more control of the way I shift back and forth between images. It's so true that we don't like to have our views upset. I can see why we try so hard to stick to our own "truths" even in the face of contradictions.
> —GAIL, PRESCHOOL TEACHER

> These activities really made me look at what I take for granted as truth from my own stereotypes. I realize that looking for details is very important, and I should not just assume that I know what's going on at first glance.
> —NICOLE, EARLY CHILDHOOD EDUCATION (ECE) STUDENT

Sample Observation Display

Learning to see in new ways requires you to notice the details. Rather than just reacting to what you see, choose a lens through which to study the details. A useful lens is to imagine the possibilities of how children's amazing, flexible brains may see the world. In the following story, teacher Dana demonstrates how she uses her lively mind to imagine what four-month-old Dominick may be experiencing as she offers him an invitation to notice the magical dancing light she provides. Dana has changed how she sees the children and her work because she practices seeing intentionally.

Dominick and the Dancing Lights

Dominick, while you were engaged in tummy time, I thought it would be a great time to introduce you to the magic of light. I placed flashlights on the floor near you with a couple of toys around you. You noticed the light reflecting on the toy closest to the flashlight, but that didn't seem to draw your attention. So I took the flashlight and began to move it back and forth between two toys. That's when the excitement started!

You began to kick your legs and make sounds as if you were talking about what you were seeing. You moved your head to follow the light as it danced around the room. When the dancing light stopped near you, you reached toward it.

Dominick, were you trying to grab the light? Or were you reaching for the glowing toy as the light shined on it? When you were cooing, were you talking about what you saw? Or were you asking, "What is that? How does that make the toy glow? Does that happen to everything light touches?" I think you may have many questions and answers for me to notice as you learn about the wonder of light.

Dominick, I've always known that children like you have a great capacity to learn, but I didn't realize how much you could learn from me and I could learn from you. I've changed how I see and do everything. I'm doing many of the same activities, but I'm doing them in a different way. Rather than focusing on an activity, I focus on you and your experience of the activity. I've learned to try to think about what you might be experiencing. I know that you see many

things that I don't see. I pose questions to myself, asking if I saw something for the first time, what would I see? I might wonder, "How did that happen? How did that get there?" I get so excited because I see the look of wonder on your face and how your body responds excitedly, and I know we are connected.

—DANA, TEACHER

Chapter 3

Study Session: Observing for Children's Perspectives

If you have a child of two or three, or can borrow one, let her give you beginning lessons in looking. It takes just a few minutes. Ask the child to come from the front of the house to the back and closely observe her small journey. It will be full of pauses, circling, touching, and picking up in order to smell, shake, taste, rub, and scrape. The child's eyes won't leave the ground, and every piece of paper, every scrap, every object along the way will be a new discovery.

It does not matter if this is familiar territory—the same house, the same rug and chair. To the child, the journey of this particular day, with its special light and sound, has never been made before. So the child treats the situation with the open curiosity and attention that it deserves.

The child is quite right.

—CORITA KENT AND JAN STEWARD

Learning Goals for This Study Session

In this study session, you will

- practice looking closely at the things around you
- recall and reflect on a favorite childhood memory
- study the elements of childhood
- practice seeing children's perspectives and capabilities

Reflect on the Quote

Corita Kent and Jan Steward remind us that it is valuable for adults to remember the world from a child's point of view. Reread Kent and Steward's quote above with these questions in mind:

1   What is your reaction to this quote?

2   Do you have any recent experiences that you can relate to it?

3   What is something you have learned or been reminded of by a child that you wouldn't have noticed if the child hadn't shown or told you?

Read this teacher's reflection to spark your thinking and discussion about this quote. You may want to reflect on this on your own or in a discussion with a partner or small group.

To me this quote means I go about my daily life rather quickly. A lot of times it involves going the same route, walking the same street, greeting the same people, and passing the same houses, trees, or flowers. As I keep my eyes straight ahead and my mind a million miles away, I miss the small wonders of every day, the wonders that really make life precious. If I take off my blinders and my filters, the detail and the wonder will fill my senses and I will truly see! When I'm with children, I will observe and take in the small wonders of what the children are doing and seeing, and I'll know I've seen something truly precious.—SHERRY, ECE STUDENT

Art of Awareness Activity

Looking Closely

Take a walk around outdoors. Approach this walk as if you are seeing things for the first time, the way Corita Kent and Jan Steward describe a child's journey in the quote you reflected on. As you walk, keep your attention on the ground. Pause, circle, touch, and pick things up to smell, taste, rub, scrape, or bend. Notice shadows, light, and sounds. Choose something you are drawn to and spend a few extra minutes exploring it. Draw a sketch of it and write a description of all the details and your reactions to what you observed. Talk with a partner about what you discovered.

Learn to See Childhood as a Significant Part of the Life Cycle

Children see so much that we miss. Once we become adults, two of the things we miss out on most are who children really are and the value of childhood. Parents and teachers who spend each day with children often focus on who the children will become, rather than who they are in the here and now. If we are to overcome this adult vision of the world, we must start to notice the remarkable point of view of young children and the important work of childhood.

Children are constantly demonstrating what they have learned and what they know how to do. While their expressions may seem naive or undeveloped, they actually represent children's incredible urge to make sense of the world. Current research shows that children's brains are very different from adults' brains. Children actually hear, see, and feel more intensely than adults do (Gopnik 2010). The more we learn about child development and the implications of brain research, the more it's confirmed that childhood is a profoundly significant time of life.

As we observe children pursuing their interest in play and conversations, we have to recognize that these moments are the bricks and mortar of developing lives. Witnessing and participating in this process provides adults with a larger view of ourselves in the life cycle. Our lives are enriched and expanded when we pause to appreciate the experience of childhood.

When we take time to recall favorite childhood memories of our own, we value more fully what we see children doing. It is useful to think back regularly to fond memories of your own childhood. These memories provide continual insight into what children need from you. The next activity offers you the opportunity to explore a childhood memory.

Practice with a Favorite Childhood Memory

You can do this activity on your own, with a partner, or in a small group. First, gather your thoughts and recall a favorite memory from your childhood. Use the following questions to help you explore the details of your memory:

- Where did the events you recall take place?
- What was in the environment?
- What were the sensory aspects of this place?
- What did it look like, smell like, sound like, feel like, taste like?
- Who else was there?
- What feelings do you associate with this memory?
- What was your sense of time?
- What skills and competencies were a part of this experience? How have they influenced who you are today?

As you reflect on your memory and perhaps hear those of others, consider the themes that are being expressed. Most people's childhood memories share some of these common elements:

- spending time outdoors with nature and/or animals
- being inventive; transforming found objects into props for play
- taking risks, wanting power, adventures, and physical challenges
- having lots of time to explore without adult interference
- getting messy, dirty, and sometimes into mischief
- working alone and with others, solving problems and resolving conflicts
- being involved in meaningful work, often with adults
- enjoying celebrations and family or community gatherings

It's not surprising that these themes come up among adults over and over. These are some of the most significant experiences of childhood. They influence children's development and learning, so it is important for teachers to be able to recognize and value these experiences. One of the easiest ways to recognize the value they have for children is to remember the value they had for us when we were children. As you become a keen observer of the children you work with, you will also see the value of these experiences for them.

Remembering our own childhood helps us keep it at the center of our thinking and planning. It helps us to uncover the child's point of view in the observations we make.

Observation Practice

Here are a few observation stories to help you practice uncovering the child's point of view.

Hello, Shadow!

It was a beautiful sunny day late in the spring. Two-year-old Adam chose to explore a dried-up mud puddle in the center of the yard. He scratched at the ground with his fingers and used the palm of his hand to pat the dirt, making a little dust cloud. Adam giggled and continued to scratch at the ground. Suddenly Adam stopped. He wiggled his fingers on one hand as it hovered just above the space. Adam stared at the ground and periodically turned his hand toward his face and wiggled his fingers. With his hand positioned above the ground once more, Adam wiggled his fingers again. "Hello, shadow!" Adam greeted his shadow with a friendly wave.

—SHELLY, TODDLER TEACHER

Consider these questions as you reflect on this story:

1   How does Adam show us his interest in the shadows?

2   What clues does he give about what he notices about the shadow?

3   What might he be understanding or trying to figure out with this shadow exploration?

Although toddlers like Adam don't use many words, they have many ways of telling us what they are noticing and trying to understand. Adam uses gestures and actions as his language, showing us his attention to detail by interacting with the shadow using his body and hands. Grown-ups often overlook toddlers' seemingly small experiences, when in fact close observation shows us the complexity of what is going on.

From the time children are born and maybe before, they are naturally equipped to use their ever-developing skills to learn about the world around them. They are born scientists and powerful communicators in pursuing and calling attention to their needs and interests. Some adults have to discipline themselves to pay attention to these small moments. Others are easily drawn to these expressions of toddlers' experience. Which is true for you? What might help you begin to notice more?

Making Things Right

Jason is six years old. Each day, he goes through the same routines when he gets to his after-school program. First, he goes around and greets everyone, addressing them by their first and last names with a monotone cadence: "Rhonda Black," "Pam Verner," "Tracy Custer." He then checks all the doors in the room, and if any of them are open, he closes them. On the days when the lights are off, he turns them

on. Once he has completed these tasks, he goes to the block area and stays there as long as the teachers will let him.

Jason doesn't have many close friendships or get involved in activities with others. Yet the children know that he is able to build incredible block structures, and they often ask for his assistance. He responds to their requests and then returns to solitary activities. Typically, this means building elaborate block cities or airports and lining up all the cars in rows until he has used every one.—CINDY, TEACHER

Look closely at the details of the story and the photo to see what you can learn about Jason.

1   What are some consistent patterns in his behavior?

2   What is he good at?

3   What does he seem to enjoy?

4   What can you say about his relationships with others?

Do some reflective writing or discussing to explore Jason's capabilities and perspectives.

Jason has been assessed as a child with special needs. Falling back on this label can lead people around him to miss who he is and ignore the remarkable things he knows and can do. While it's true children like Jason need some special consideration, the starting point for working with any child should be recognizing the way he sees the world and the strengths he brings to himself and others.

If your response to Jason is one of sympathy or a desire to fix him, can you transform it to one of curiosity and eagerness to know more about how the world looks through his eyes? What questions might you ask yourself to help you focus on his capabilities? How might you help the other children to marvel at his abilities?

Wrestling with the Wind

Nick immediately had an idea for using the sparkly red fabric that he found on the playground. He decided to cover the table with it. This wasn't an easy task. The wind was blowing steadily, and the fabric moved and swayed in response as Nick tried to lay it on the table. He attempted many strategies to get the fabric to lay flat. He leaned over and used his body to hold it down, but when he got up, the fabric immediately blew away. He tried shaking the fabric to fling it over the table, but to no avail. The fabric kept blowing up against his body. Next, he pulled one corner of the fabric at a time. But still the fabric blew with the wind. When the wind subsided a bit, Nick was able to stretch the fabric taut over the table. When he had accomplished his goal, he swept the fabric off the table with a flair and began to twirl around, dancing with the wind and the fabric.

—KIM, TEACHER

Use the following questions to focus on Nick's experience in this observation:

1   What is the essence of this experience from Nick's point of view?

2   What does Nick understand and know how to do?

3   What is Nick exploring, experimenting with, or trying to figure out?

4   What does Nick find frustrating?

5   How does Nick feel about himself?

When you look closely and examine the details of their actions from their point of view, you discover how ingenious and motivated children are when they initiate and pursue their own ideas and interests. Nick used flexible thinking and problem solving to meet the challenge he set for himself. His persistence is commendable.

Take Another Look

Each day in your teaching, you have the opportunity to notice children's competence and creativity, even when they are engaging in activities that may challenge you. If you approach your time with them as a researcher, filling your mind with questions rather than labels or judgments, you will discover a new way of seeing them. As you begin to cultivate this mind-set, try the following activities to heighten your awareness.

Practice Taking the Child's Perspective

Observe a child in your setting who is involved in ordinary, self-directed play. Use the questions below to help you understand the child's perspective.

1   What is the essence of this experience from the child's point of view?

2   What does the child know and know how to do?

3   What is the child exploring, experimenting with, or trying to figure out?

4   What does the child find frustrating?

5   How does the child feel about herself?

Try to Do What You See Children Doing

You can learn to see children's perspectives in very powerful ways if you observe them closely and then try imitating what you see them doing. Notice the details of how children use materials, approach a task, or solve a problem, and literally copy what they do. You can do this side by side with the children by asking their permission to try their ideas and then describe the details of what you are doing and noticing as you work. Children will often engage with you, giving you more insight into their points of view. They may repeat or expand their actions or tell you more about what's on their minds, as the following story suggests.

Anthony and the Paintbrush

Twenty-month-old Anthony was working with a paintbrush and watercolor. I sat next to him, watching for a while. I didn't want to intrude on his focus, so I waited until I observed a pattern in what he was doing. This indicated to me that he had possibly made a discovery that he was repeating. I noticed he was using the paintbrush very carefully to make small marks of paint, so I picked up my own brush and suggested I wanted to try what he was doing. As I worked, I described the details of our brushes and how they moved as we worked.

I also pointed to and noticed the marks we were making with the brushes. Anthony immediately examined his brush and studied his actions as he made the marks again. He continued doing this same action over and over again, covering the page with the paint marks.

Lily, sitting next to him, was listening and watching what Anthony and I did together. She quickly moved the jar of blue watercolor near her and began to try Anthony's idea as well. Anthony protested with a toddler squeal when he noticed that Lily had taken the jar. I suggested, "Look, Anthony, Lily liked your idea and wants to try it. She's making small marks of paint on her paper just like you did, and she needs the blue paint to do it." He easily gave up his desire for the jar of paint and watched her actions closely. They willingly began to move the jar back and forth between them, continuing to make the marks and watching as they worked. I was delighted by how imitating and naming the details of Anthony's and Lily's individual actions helped them see and connect with each other. This experience helped me understand that even at this young age, children have the desire and ability to cooperate. If I see their skills and competencies and offer these back to them, amazing things happen.
                                            —DEB, CHILD CARE TEACHER

You can also seek children's perspectives by trying out what children do when you are not with them. This often gives you insight into activities and behaviors you may find challenging, as reflected in the following story.

Buzzing around the Water Table

With an endless fountain of youthful energy and curiosity, an exuberant group of boys buzz around the pipes and tubes at the water table. "Fill up the bucket so the water can come out!" "Turn it on! . . . Ha! It's on, it's on!" When all the busy hands cause the pipes to come apart and cut off the water supply, I hear Ryder's voice ringing out loudly and clearly, "Nobody panic! I know what to do!" And, true to his word, he reassembles the pipes and the play resumes as enthusiastically as ever.

Admittedly, when I first saw them descend upon our new pipe and hose structure, the thought that came to mind was, "This is absolute chaos!" But after looking more closely I saw that the boys were playing with real intention. No one had explained to them how the pipes work. Instead, the group experimented with each part of the contraption until they had a clear understanding of how it worked. With purpose the boys deduced that they needed to pour water into the bucket, use the valves to direct the flow of water, and then aim the appropriate hose in order to fill the intended container. Was it a lively affair? Certainly. Chaotic? Well, maybe a little, but it was the controlled kind that often makes exploration the most fun.

I wanted to get more insight into the children's exuberance so I examined the details of my observations to try out for myself what the children did with the water. To my surprise and excitement, I had a wonderful time working with the water and pipes in this way. Because of this experience, I'm recommitted to helping the children continue with this water activity, and dive in with them to help negotiate the chaos!

—MICHAEL, CHILD CARE TEACHER

Crop Photos to See What Children See

Study children's perspectives by cropping and enlarging photos of their activities. Cameras and digital technology are so easy to use. They provide abundant opportunities for teachers to take photos and use them to study children's ideas and points of view. As you take photos for study, it is helpful to zoom in to focus on the children in relationship with each other and with materials. Begin by taking a photo of the child in the larger context of the situation and then zoom in on the child's hands, face, and body language. As you study the photos, you can highlight aspects you want to see more clearly. Then crop the photos, cutting out the background and enlarging the elements you want to emphasize for study. In the example here of the child exploring cornstarch and water, you can see the details of the texture, shapes, movement, and reflection of light on the substance that she appears to be noticing. Studying photos in this way allows you to see the purposeful actions children use to explore their world. When you see and study children at work in these ways, you enhance your view of their competence and take children more seriously. This strategy also helps you step into their experiences and share in the wonders of the world they see.

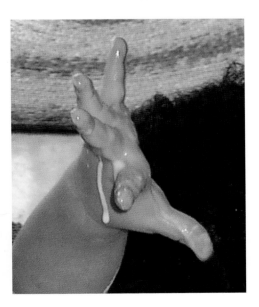

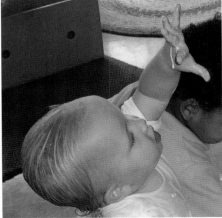

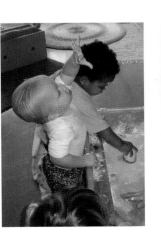

Notice How Children See Adults

Children have laserlike attention for everything adults do and say. They are skillful social scientists—learning about themselves, relationships, and the world by carefully observing the people around them. In fact, children are primed to see us. Infants are born with the ability to see best at a distance of eight to fourteen inches, the perfect distance for gazing up from the arms of their mothers, fathers, and caregivers. It's the perfect distance to begin to build connections and relationships and learn from seeing us. If we are fascinated with how children see the world, then reflecting about how they see us is useful.

- Do our faces show delight or consternation?
- Do our hands soothe or scold?
- Do our voices invite singing together or command silence?
- Do our bodies overwhelm children with our size and power or wrap them up in comfort?

As keen observers, children notice the smallest details of our body language, tone of voice, and movements. Our interactions and presence have a powerful impact on how children view themselves and us. With this power comes an opportunity—as well as a tremendous responsibility—for us to use it well. Notice in the following example how Simone reflects on these ideas.

Simone and the Swing

Simone was sitting on a swing, observing children, when a verbal and assertive child approached her with a disturbed look on his face.

"Hey, Miss Simone, you can't do that," he exclaimed. "You can't sit on the swing!"

Surprised and perplexed by his statement, Simone asked, "Why can't I sit on the swing?"

"Because you're a teacher," he explained very matter-of-factly. "You're a grown-up, and grown-ups can't go on swings." And with that, he ran off to play in the sprinklers.

Later, Simone reflected on this encounter. "I wonder why he thought teachers, or grown-ups, couldn't sit on the swing. Is it because of the size of grown-up bodies that he felt adults couldn't fit on a structure designed for children, that there is a physical limitation due to our size? Did he believe that while our big bodies can do many things, there are some games or activities that are especially reserved for children? Or had he come to expect adults not to engage in childlike behavior? Did the adults in his life often use the fact that they're grown up as a reason not to play as much, or as vigorously—a reason to avoid getting sweaty or dirty?

How does the way we use our size, experience, and abilities affect the way children view us? I wonder what other subliminal messages we send to children just in the way we carry ourselves.

—SIMONE, TEACHER

More Things to Do

It will take continual practice to cultivate these ways of seeing and being with children. Here are activities to contribute to your development.

Explore Your Current View of Children

Read the following statements and look at the accompanying photo, alone or with others, and explore how you see this child. Consider which of these statements comes closest to representing your view. There is no right answer here, and in many ways, each of them is true. Just reflect on which view most guides your own behavior.

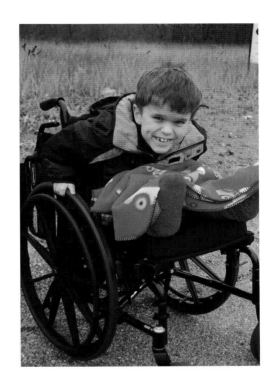

- Children are vulnerable and need protection.
- Children do fine on their own, and adults should stay out of their way.
- Children need strong guidance and direction from adults in their lives.
- Children benefit from adults who both support and challenge them.

All of these statements have simple truths to them, yet how we see children is not so simple. Our view of children affects everything we do, how we respond, and what we offer children. If we see children as competent—able to make important choices for themselves and to learn in meaningful, self-directed ways—then we will offer them more possibilities for their growth and development. This is true for typically developing children as well as children with special needs. Observing closely for the details of children's skills and competencies and trying to see their points of view help us to respond in these valuable ways.

Explore Images of Childhood in Children's Literature

From *Winnie the Pooh* to *Oliver Twist*, images of childhood engage our imaginations and emotions. They also can help us deepen our commitment to providing rich childhood experiences in our programs. Find a selection of children's literature to study. Compare three or four books, on your own or with others. Some possibilities include:

Mama, Do You Love Me? by Barbara M. Joosse

The Runaway Bunny by Margaret Wise Brown

I'm Not Cute! by Jonathan Allen

Roxaboxen by Alice McLerran

Tell Me Something Happy before I Go to Sleep by Joyce Dunbar

As you reflect on each story, consider the following questions:

1   What childhood themes are portrayed in this story?

2   How is this experience contributing to the children's sense of self and belonging?

3   What elements from this story do you want to create for the children you work with?

Sample Observation Display

Notice in the following story how Jesly reflects on what she sees Fini doing in the basket. She notices Fini's point of view, and instead of stopping what Fini is exploring, she delights in the unique idea Fini has and how she has transferred knowledge from one spinning object to this new experience. The format of this story is inspired by an approach to assessing children created by early childhood educators in New Zealand. It is called a Learning Story and is written directly to the child, with a detailed observation of what happened and an analysis of the meaning and the possibilities this experience provides.

Spinning Fini

What happened:
Dear Fini,
I saw you using the large metal top, pushing it up and down to make it spin. You leaned back to watch how it was spinning as you manipulated it. Then you took all of the tops out of the basket. The next thing I noticed was you climbing in the basket. You held yourself up by holding on to the sides of the basket and used your legs to move your body and the basket in a circular motion. You worked slowly at first, trying to keep your balance as your body would slide forward in

the basket. You resettled yourself in the center of the basket to gain your balance. Fini, you realized you couldn't make the basket spin if you weren't sitting exactly in the middle of the basket. As you figured out how to control your body in the wobbly basket, you were able to use your legs to turn around, just like the metal tops. The more you figured things out, the faster you could spin. You kept spinning for a long time.

What we think this means:
I wonder if, by examining the metal tops spinning, that gave you the idea to try to spin yourself in the basket. I thought it was so clever of you to come up with this brilliant idea. Some of the things you were learning through this play:

You were able to observe the action of the top and think about how to apply this to your own body.

You were able to problem solve throughout the experience as you adjusted your body to do what you had in your mind.

You were able to use trial and error to manipulate your body and the basket to make it spin.

You expressed your creativity by using the basket in this way.

You also showed us how coordinated you are with your body.

What opportunities does this experience hold for you and your teachers?
I realized that often I stop children from using materials in an unusual way, like you did with the basket. I learned that if I wait and watch before I jump in, amazing learning can happen.

I want to continue to support you to use materials in these creative ways.

I want to offer you more obstacles to challenge your competent physical self, such as a balancing board and more ways to spin.

—JESLY, EARLY CHILDHOOD TEACHER

Chapter 4

Study Session: Observing Children's Lively Minds

We used to think that babies and young children were irrational,
egocentric, and amoral. Their thinking and experience were concrete,
immediate, and limited. In fact, psychologists and neuroscientists have
discovered that babies not only learn more, but imagine more, care
more, and experience more than we would ever have thought possible.
In some ways, young children are actually smarter, more imaginative,
more caring, and even more conscious than adults are.
—ALISON GOPNIK

Learning Goals for This Study Session

In this study session, you will

- expand your capacity for focus and memory
- increase the flexibility of your brain
- practice seeing the details of children's lively minds at work
- deepen your respect and appreciation for children's innate ability to focus and learn

Reflect on the Quote

Alison Gopnik proposes a provocative idea: babies may actually be smarter than adults. Consider the following questions as you reflect on the quote:

1 What is your response to the idea that young children have more capacity than they are given credit for?

2 What are some of the experiences you have had when you were amazed by a young child's mind?

3 What do you think of the concept that young children may actually be smarter than adults?

Work alone or with a group, using the following teacher's thoughts to promote your own thinking.

Babies never cease to amaze me! Their ability to communicate with adults and other children is fascinating, especially considering their lack of spoken language. When I first met my best friend's baby, then twelve months old, she was enjoying cereal as a snack. She allowed me to feed her the pieces of cereal, nodding and giggling whenever I said "Yum!" or "Tasty!" Occasionally, she'd ask for more using sign language. When I said, "I wish *I* had a delicious snack like yours," she reached into the cup and began feeding me her cereal. We continued to share her cereal, taking turns feeding each other until it was finished, when she happily signed, "All done!" It was probably the most precious and heartfelt moment I ever shared with a person so young.—SIMONE, EARLY CHILDHOOD TEACHER

I wonder if as we age, our minds are slowly narrowing—that we may be becoming literally more closed-minded day by day. I believe that very young children are infinitely more talented learners than we are as adults, and if we are equating the ability to learn quickly and to learn well with intelligence, I absolutely believe that babies are smarter than we grown-ups. As such, we are incredibly fortunate in the position that we are in, as adults colearning with young children. We have the opportunity every day to be stunned by the depth and complexity of young children's thinking as they work to decipher the subtleties of things we take for granted—perhaps allowing us to counteract some of that narrowing and open our own minds to new possibilities. What an incredible gift!—JESS, EARLY CHILDHOOD TEACHER

Children amaze me. They are both mirrors and sponges. They reflect our understanding of them. You can always tell when children feel honored and understood by adults. You can see it in their eyes and in the relationships they have with you. Children soak up their experiences and wring them back out, making connections that would not be obvious to adults. That's what's amazing to me about a child's mind.—UWIMANA, EARLY CHILDHOOD TEACHER

Art of Awareness Activity

The following activities will help you expand your ability to focus and enhance your lively mind.

Use Your Peripheral Vision

Look straight ahead and try to see everything you can, both in front of you and at the side (this is your peripheral vision). Don't move your eyes or head. When you are done, see if you can remember everything you noticed and write it all down. Share what you discovered with others. This will force you to use your memory and stimulate the chemicals in your brain that are important for focus and memory.

Try Using Your Other Hand

If you are like most people, you can only use one of your hands with any coordination. We call it being right-handed or left-handed. One hand is dominant for most people. Make a game of using your less-dominant hand to do things such as writing or drawing. This challenges your brain to use a part of your body differently than it's used to.

Learn to See Childhood as a Time of Unprecedented Learning

In the last decade, there has been a revolution in our understanding of brain development and learning in young children. Young children have a motivation and capacity for learning that is far greater than we have understood before. Research suggests that children's drive to learn is as strong as their drive to eat. Policies, programs, and practices on behalf of children's learning have yet to reflect the research. Most early learning initiatives emphasize getting children ready to learn. These programs emphasize assessment, standards, and curriculum models that focus on teaching children to meet identified outcomes. They do not enhance or maximize the eager dispositions and huge capacity children already bring to the learning process. The misguided focus on academics and school readiness keeps many early childhood teachers from seeing children's intrinsically lively minds at work. When teachers are overly concerned about teaching the alphabet and other isolated skills and facts, they may miss children's serious approaches to tasks and their voracious quests to understand the world around them. As Lilian Katz suggests, children are more apt to be interested in intellectual pursuits than academic lessons. Observing children for these intellectual pursuits helps teachers learn to value, respond, and plan more meaningful learning experiences for children.

Merriam-Webster's Collegiate Dictionary defines *intellectual* as "given to study, reflection, and speculation" and "engaged in activity requiring the creative use of the intellect." Obviously it is important for children to learn appropriate skills and tasks. But rather than overly focusing on these goals, teachers can claim and enjoy the responsibility to protect and enhance children's natural gift for learning. Teachers can help children remain energized about the wonders around them. Young children already have a powerful drive to learn all the time, so your job is to find ways to really see, appreciate, and further their intellectual pursuits.

Practice Expanding the Flexibility of Your Brain

One of the amazing capacities of children's brains is their ability to use ordinary objects in a variety of ways. Here's a way for you to expand the flexibility of your brain.

- Work alone or preferably with a group so you can share your brainpower and reflections.

- On a piece of paper, write the numbers 1 through 100 in a column with a space next to each number to record your ideas.

- Find a familiar object such as your keys, a fork, or a scarf.

- Brainstorm at least 100 different ways you could use the object, and record each idea you come up with.

- Time how long it takes you to complete this task.

- Discuss the following questions:

  1 How difficult or easy was it for you to come up with new ideas?

  2 What thinking and learning strategies did you use to think of new ideas?

  3 How would you assess your ability to be a creative, flexible thinker?

The following sample observations illustrate how children think in flexible ways.

Nicolas Explores Vibrations

Nicolas was introduced to a battery-operated back massager. When his teacher, Shelly, first gave it to him, she had turned it on so it was vibrating and making a buzzing sound. This made Nicolas giggle! He immediately took hold of the massager and started to drive it around the floor. Then Shelly turned off the massager and gave it back to Nicolas. He seemed puzzled at first, as if he were trying to figure out why the massager had stopped working. He turned it over and examined each side for clues. Nicolas finally found the power switch and turned it on. To his delight, the massager began to bounce around the floor again! As the battery power began to wear down, the massager got slower and quieter until it finally stopped. When this happened the first time, Nicolas immediately pressed the power switch. He seemed

a little surprised when the massager did not turn on again. He stood up and walked over to the table, placed the massager on it, and pressed the button again. Surprisingly, it came on, but just for a few seconds. Puzzled again, he took the massager over to the carpet and pressed the button. Again, the massager turned on for a few seconds! Every time the massager stopped, Nicolas found a new place to try the power button again. Shelly tried to offer some help to him by suggesting they open it and check the batteries, but he refused, clutching the massager tightly as he explored other things in the room.

—SHELLY, TODDLER TEACHER

Immersed in Puffy Balls

Jamison eagerly approached the table filled with soft, colorful puffy balls. All of her senses were alert as she explored the balls. She picked up one of the balls and looked at it closely. She put it up to her nose as if to smell it and even put it on her tongue. Then she squished the fuzzy ball in her hand and immediately leaned in and put both hands into the pile. She immersed her arms and body into the abundant pile of balls and began swishing them around the tub, watching them move. Then she discovered she could throw the balls. She watched delightedly as the balls bounced and rolled all over the floor. At one point, we showed her that she could use a spoon to scoop the balls into a container. She focused on filling the containers but only to quickly launch the balls into the air and all over the floor again.   —JESLY, EARLY CHILDHOOD TEACHER

Take Children's Actions Seriously

It's easy to dismiss their explorations, because children move quickly, make messes, and put themselves in seemingly risky situations. To take their activities seriously, it is useful to develop the practice of waiting to determine what the thinking might be underneath their actions before you jump into a situation. When you do this, you come to see that with most everything children do, they have something in mind. They have a purpose or question they are pursuing. When you take even their smallest actions seriously, you will be astonished at children's deep engagement with the simple wonders around them. You will notice they are studying and speculating, engrossed in each moment.

See Children's Capacity for Learning

Research shows that children are born with many intrinsic capacities for learning about the world they live in:

Strong, instinctive curiosity: Children have an inborn drive to continually explore, experiment, and make discoveries. This drive gives children a huge capacity for focus and concentration as well as persistence.

Flexible brains: Research shows that because young children's brains have what scientists call *plasticity*, they actually see more, hear more, experience more, and feel more strongly than adults. With this comes the power to observe closely and see details. It also gives children the gift of a fluid imagination and aptitude to see multiple possibilities for objects and situations.

The scientific method: When you observe children closely, you see they actually use a form of the scientific method that most scientists use. They begin with a question—"Why?"—and then collect information to answer it. Children observe, explore and investigate, sort and classify, then formulate a hypothesis. They test the hypothesis and analyze what happens. They try things again and again to consolidate their understandings. Based on the data, they either disprove the hypothesis and start the process again, or they formulate a final hypothesis or come to a conclusion.

Observation Practice

As you study the following observations, look closely for how children are using their instinctive capacities, lively minds, and flexible brains to learn.

Organizing Cups

Olivia approached the table of cups and sparkly objects with a serious look on her face and got to work. First, she lined cups into two rows and then placed a diamond in each cup. She said earnestly, "Looks like ice." Next, she removed the diamonds and placed a small letter in each cup. Then she stacked the cups carefully in her arms and ventured around the room, collecting more cups as she went along. After a short while, she brought the cups back to the table, where she lined up the shortest cups first and filled them with different shapes. Next, she lined up the larger cups and filled them halfway up with letters. She spotted more empty cups across the table and added them to her line, putting letters in those cups as well. Her face lit up with excitement when she took a step back to look at what she had accomplished.   —SUE, PRESCHOOL TEACHER

Use the following questions to study Olivia's intellectual pursuits.

1   Which details in the story tell you what Olivia has on her mind and what she is trying to accomplish?

2   What dispositions toward learning does Olivia exhibit in this observation?

3   What learning concepts can you identify in her investigation?

Abundant Buttons

Jake spent the entire morning captivated by the table filled with hundreds of buttons. His initial ideas for exploring the buttons were different from all the other children's. Rather than comparing and sorting buttons, which was what the other children did, Jake seemed to delight in exploring the buttons as a sensory material. He put his hands inside the bag of buttons and ran his fingers through them again and again. He enjoyed how the buttons moved and felt. He noticed the sounds the buttons made as he swished them around. After a long time exploring the slick, smooth movement of the buttons, Jake decided he wanted to gather all of the buttons and put them in the bag. This was a big job, because there were a lot of buttons, but he was determined to fill up the bag!

Jake faced the challenge of how to transport the most buttons to the bag at one time. He tried out a number of innovative ways to solve the problem. First, he used his hands to pick up the buttons, but he wanted to move more of them than his hands could hold. Next, he tried picking up buttons with a piece of paper, but they kept sliding off the sides before he got them to the bag. Finally, he figured out how to scoop the buttons onto a tray, gather them together in a pile, and pour them into the bag. He was thrilled with his success and immediately dumped the buttons from the bag and started the process over again. Jake filled and dumped several times, delighting each time he succeeded in this big task!

—Dianne, Angela, Nicole, Wendy, Debbie, and Norma, preschool teacher community of practice

Use the following questions to guide your discussion about Jake's lively mind.

1   What skills and dispositions toward learning did Jake demonstrate?

2   What details did you notice about Jake's use of the buttons?

3   What new ideas about buttons did you get from how Jake used them?

Open-ended materials offered in abundance, like the ones described in these two observations, are the perfect tools for children to use in exercising their abilities to think flexibly, imagine many possibilities, generate hypotheses, and solve problems. They are simple materials, yet they invite children to use them in complex ways. Olivia and Jake both show us there are many more possibilities for learning with these simple materials than we realize. They remind us to observe the details of children's intellectual pursuits and remain open to seeing the value of their ideas. If we observe closely, many rich learning experiences will unfold before our eyes.

Engage with Children in Intellectual Pursuits

Teacher agendas often get in the way of children's lively minds. We stop their pursuits in the names of safety, group management, teaching skills or facts, and our own ideas about what makes sense. There might be moments in the observation stories of Olivia and Jake when a teacher might interrupt the learning. Olivia might be stopped from wandering the room to find all of the cups. Jake might be told that the buttons are for sorting. When you observe closely, you see the value. Then you can join in with the children and help expand their natural capacities. Read the following Sample Observation to hear another story of a teacher observing a child's amazing mind at work.

A Hidden Technique

Uwimana was in the art room, working with the children on a special canvas that was offered for a group project. She was making sure that the children who were engaged in painting were careful not to paint over the work previously done by their peers, so everyone could be represented in the project. She noticed that every time she looked up, different children were painting the canvas and the colors had changed drastically. She began to remind children to paint around the images they saw and not over them, but still the children used the paint to paint over one another's work. The canvas went from blue to brown to orange and then to a bluish brown. One of the children, Yara, watched as another child painted on the canvas. She looked on as different colors were added to the painting. There really wasn't any more

space to add paint to the canvas; still, Yara said that she was interested in painting. She asked for the color green. A couple of moments later, she had painted the entire canvas green. All of the other colors were gone. Uwimana was going to remind Yara of the agreement about the painting project when she saw Yara take the other end of the paintbrush and scratch it down the center of the canvas. She moved the tip all over and in different directions as she began scribing with the paintbrush on the canvas. She was using the paintbrush in an unconventional way, making a different kind of design, and her actions revealed all of the colors that had been painted over. Yara scratched and scratched until the canvas had a plethora of different colors showing from beneath the green paint.

—UWIMANA, EARLY CHILDHOOD TEACHER

Here are Uwimana's reflections about her observation:

Yara watched while other children painted on the canvas, she observed as they painted over one another's images, and she listened as I reminded the children to create their images on the available space on the canvas. The technique she used in scribing the paintbrush on the canvas allowed for the painting done by her peers to gleam through. It was as if she heard me and saw what the children were doing and came to a compromise that worked for everyone. Is it possible that a hidden technique was used by all of the children participating in creating images on the canvas? They seemed to approach the canvas with a specific goal in mind that did not always include preserving the work of their peers. There were times in which the children were very careful; they painted around the work of their peers and reminded each other to do also. I am learning to watch, wait, and listen. I'm also learning to revisit our rules and agreements. Just because something is agreed upon doesn't mean it can't be revisited or updated. Amazing things can happen.

—UWIMANA, EARLY CHILDHOOD TEACHER

Take Another Look

Because our adult brains are so very different from those of the children we work with, it takes practice to keep up with their lively minds. When you understand that children are voracious learners, pursuing new information, knowledge, and skills every minute, then you will approach their ideas and actions with respect, curiosity, and awe. Use the following activities to see these amazing people more clearly.

Observe Children's Natural Capacities and Gifts for Learning

When you are with your group of children, spend time each day observing and documenting the details of their innate learning abilities. Take notes and photos when you see children engaged in the following:

- using their strong, instinctive curiosity

- showing their capacity to focus and concentrate

- persisting in a task or activity and trying something again and again

- drawing on their flexible brains to observe closely and see details

- using their imagination and aptitude to see multiple possibilities

- practicing the scientific method as they ask questions, explore and investigate, sort and classify, form hypotheses, test them through observation and trial and error, analyze what happens, form new hypotheses, problem solve, try things over again and again, and finally consolidate their understandings and draw conclusions

Notice when you are tempted to stop intellectual pursuits. Become aware of moments when you are watching children and your instinct is to stop them because of health or safety or your own idea about what makes sense. Before involving yourself in the activity, watch the children closely and reflect on the following questions:

1   What curiosity, questions, hypotheses, or ideas may be on the children's minds?

2   What do you value about what you see the children doing?

3   How might you join in or support the children's intellectual pursuit in this situation?

More Things to Do

Here are some other ways you can further sharpen your observation skills and expand your ability to understand children's lively minds.

Study the Work of Alison Gopnik

Alison Gopnik is a researcher and professor of psychology at the University of California–Berkeley. She has done extensive studies, writing and speaking about the most current research on young children's brain development and learning. Her books *The Philosophical Baby* and *The Scientist in the Crib* offer comprehensive, accessible information as well as astounding insight into the amazing world of young children. Visit her website at www.alisongopnik .com. All of us who work with young children need to learn what she knows, as there are huge implications for our practices with children!

Regularly Practice Brain-Building Exercises

The following activities come from the Internet. There are hundreds of websites with games and activities to help you increase the capacity, flexibility, and creativity of your brain. These are just a few favorites we discovered while writing this book. Do an Internet search on *brain boosters* to start your own brain-power journey, or try any of these.

Learn a language: Learning a new language has been shown to halt age-related decline in brain function. It also introduces your mind to new concepts and new ways of looking at things (in English *we are afraid*, whereas in Spanish *we have fear*). It is one of the best brain exercises.

Mindfulness exercises: Concentration and clear thinking are more or less automatic once you remove distractions. Learn to stop and watch your busy mind. As you notice things that are subtly bothering you, deal with them. This might mean making a phone call you need to make or putting things on a list so you can forget them for now. With practice, this becomes easier, and your thinking becomes more powerful.

Adjust your beliefs: Believe you are smarter, and you'll become smarter. Affirmations may work, but even better is evidence. Make a note of your successes. Tell yourself, "Hey, that was really creative" when you do something creative. When you have a good idea, make a note of it. Gather the evidence for your own intelligence, and you'll start to experience more of it.

Sample Observation Display

As you read this final story, written directly to the child, notice how Saric is fortunate to work with a skilled teacher in an environment that engages all of his natural gifts and capabilities for learning. He has become a Renaissance man at a very young age. He uses all of the tools he is offered, along with the powerful tools he already possesses, for inventing a new world with all of its possibilities. As researcher Alison Gopnik says, "Babies' minds change the world." We can see in Saric's story the truth of that statement.

I'm Making Something for Me

Dear Saric,

Recently I have seen you become more and more interested in creating and exploring different materials in the art studio. A few weeks ago, you would enter the studio quietly, find yourself a small space at the recycle table, and work on your idea. When you first started, your ideas usually involved taping one or two things together and asking for your name to be put on it. Now, just a short time later, you have become one of the art studio regulars! You walk right in and claim a space at the table, telling your friends, "I'm working here!" Your ideas have become more elaborate and detailed. You now enter the room with a plan and spend time problem solving when materials do not fit together as you had envisioned. I have noticed that your spatial understanding has increased, as you build three-dimensionally. Your ideas have become much longer, taller, and wider!

Saric, I have also watched as you have gradually become interested in other areas of the studio. You have been gluing wood, molding clay, easel painting, and drawing on transparencies. The way you have been exploring and trying new things has shown me how comfortable in our program you are becoming and the type of provocations you are interested in. I can see that you have found a new niche and know that you

are confident that you belong. You know not only the daily routine but also the routine in the studio. You work independently and with confidence on your creation, put it away, and always come back to clean. I can see and appreciate how much you respect the studio and the materials in it.

Through all of your new work, I have also seen how your assertiveness and verbal skills have grown. I hear you telling your classmates what you are making and what space you are working in and also asking questions when you need help. I am sure that soon you will be helping other children who are new to the studio.

A lot of the building that has been happening in the studio has revolved around airplanes, and I notice that you have become interested in them too. You have joined your friends in their discussions as they describe the look of their planes, adding the description of your own. Now that you have become more comfortable with the materials, I wonder if you would like to learn more about airplanes, with the intention of furthering your designs. It would be so nice to see some of your ideas and models in the *Airplane Book* that has been started by your peers in the art studio. I enjoy seeing how the shared interest in airplanes has created a bond between you and a few of your friends. I watch as you share your ideas and excitement with each other both verbally and nonverbally. Your conversations, laughs, smiles, and gestures

have all contributed to the increasing depth of your work in the studio.

Lastly, one of my favorite things to see is your smile in the studio! I can see how much fun you have as you are creating and also how much pride you feel when it is complete. Do you remember when you made a cake out of the clay? You lit up as you exclaimed, "This is a cake for me and Tachin. It is ready!" I loved seeing your imagination and creativity.

I have been so impressed with how quickly you have become an expert in the art studio. I am excited to see what other materials you will start to enjoy working with!

Love,
MISS SHEENA

Chapter 5

Study Session: Observing How Children Use Their Senses

Exploring nature with your child is largely a matter of becoming receptive to what lies all around you. It is learning again to use your eyes, ears, nostrils, and fingertips, opening up the disused channels of sensory impression. For most of us knowledge comes largely through sight, yet we look about with such unseeing eyes that we are partially blind. One way to open your eyes to unnoticed beauty is to ask yourself, "What if I had never seen this before? What if I knew I would never see it again?"
—RACHEL CARSON

Learning Goals for This Study Session

In this study session, you will

- reawaken your ability to observe with all of your senses
- examine closely using jeweler's loupes
- practice seeing the details of children's sensory exploration
- delight in and learn from children's use of their senses

Reflect on the Quote

Rachel Carson urges us to look at our ability to use our senses and see the world as children do. Use the following questions to reflect on the quote above.

1   What do you think of Carson's idea that being with children is like reawakening your senses?

2   What experiences have you had that connect to the ideas in the quote?

3   How does Carson's thinking relate to your work with children?

Discuss your ideas with a partner or small group, or do some reflective writing on your own. You might want to use this teacher's response to spark or extend your thinking.

As adults, most of us no longer think of the world as a mysterious place, and we look at the things around us with either a numb passiveness or critical judgment. Children view the world in such a different way. It is important for us to realize that children do not see things as we see them. And what a blessing it is for us to look at things in another way. It's sad that we have lost our sense of wonder, but it would be even sadder if we never noticed it was gone. We owe it to ourselves and the children we work with to close our old eyes and open new ones.—LESLIE, ECE STUDENT

Art of Awareness Activity

Seeing Up Close

Use the following activity to practice looking at the world as if you've never seen it before. This will give you a sense of what it's like to see something as children see it, and it can give you more practice in looking closely.

The Private Eye: "5X" Looking/Thinking by Analogy—A Guide to Developing the Interdisciplinary Mind by Kerry Ruef (http://www.the-private-eye.com/index.html) is a K–12 curriculum full of activities such as the one you're about to do. In it, you use jeweler's loupes to observe the world in expanded ways. You can get a jeweler's loupe either from the Private Eye folks, a local eyeglass store, or online by searching for jeweler's loupes or eye magnifiers. You could also use a high-powered magnifying glass, though it won't offer as focused a field of vision.

Follow these directions for seeing and exploring the world available to you with this simple tool.

1   Put the large end of a loupe or a magnifying glass up to your eye. Hold the object you want to examine, moving it closer and farther from your eye until it comes into focus. Forget the label or name of what you are looking at and see only the intricate details, colors, and textures.

2   Record or describe the details of what you see.

3   Draw a sketch of what you are actually seeing. Don't try to make it look like something you know the name of.

4   Reflect on and talk or write about what it reminds you of.

Here is an example of a loupe drawing and description from a teacher in an observation class.

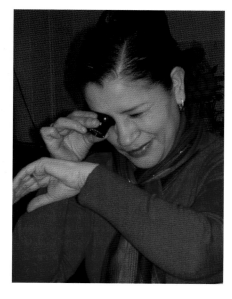

This is the part of a leaf where the stem meets the green leaf part. I could see all the veins very clearly. It kind of looked like a river system. The veins also looked like spiders' legs.

Learn to See Childhood as a World of Magic and Discovery

In the early childhood field, educators often talk about sensory exploration. Early childhood classrooms have sensory tubs and tables, lots of recipes, curriculum guides, and resources for *sensory* learning. Still, and understandably so, most often the adult response to children's sensory exploration is "What a mess!" Left to their own devices, children will mix, spill, splash, bang, crash, take apart, and widely spread the stuff of the world. When you spend your days with groups of children, it seems easier to stop them in their tracks. After all, restraining this sensory exploration means less mess, less noise, fewer germs spreading, less work, and fewer parent complaints. But read what Helen Keller said about senses; then think again:

> Smell is a potent wizard that transports us across thousands of miles and all the years we have lived. The odor of fruits waft me to my Southern home, to my childhood frolics in the peach orchard. Other odors, instantaneous and fleeting, cause my heart to dilate joyously or contract with remembered grief. Even as I think of smells, my nose is full of scents that start awake sweet memories of summers gone and ripening grain fields far away.

Children's sensory explorations provide vital discoveries about themselves and the world they live in. When you understand that children actually hear, see, and feel more intensely than adults do, you discover that your characterization of sensory experiences is rather shallow, focusing mostly on the materials you provide. When you observe closely, you can see that children are immersed in fuller aesthetic experiences in which their bodies, minds, and emotions are all engaged. For children, it's not only what they touch and mess about with, it's the physical and emotional responses to the experiences that are momentous. As they drink in the magic and wonder of the world around them, their brain pathways are making the connections that will be the foundation for a lifetime of learning and pleasure.

As Helen Keller suggests, the senses are the way we come to know about the richness of life, in the past and present. The more of these experiences children have, the better.

Adults have busy lives filled with to-do lists, schedules, and deadlines. We rush around thinking we don't have time to stop and smell the roses or marvel at a sunset. We abandon our senses and the rich aesthetic experiences available to us. We continually live in the past or the future rather than in the present with our whole selves. If we are going to value these experiences and provide them for children, we have some work to do as grown-ups. We must reawaken our ability to use our senses to experience the world. When we keep our own senses alert and our hearts and minds open, we will see and delight in children's points of view more easily. We will retain the best of our childlike qualities and stay fully alert in our adult bodies.

Practice Reawakening Your Senses

Author Henry Miller once said, "The moment one gives close attention to anything, even a blade of grass, it becomes a mysterious, awesome, indescribably magnificent world in itself." With this in mind, use the following activity to open yourself up to your senses. You can do it alone, with a partner, or in a small group.

Gather a collection of natural materials from your outdoor environment. Find items that have a variety of textures, colors, shapes, and complexity, such as leaves, twigs, stones, shells, and pods. Arrange the objects so you will be able to explore them easily. Try to let go of the name, identity, purpose, or common description of the objects. Look at them as if you've never seen them before. Use the following guidelines to focus your exploration.

- Notice how many different sounds you can make with these objects. Keep track of how many you discover, and list them.

- Explore all of the different ways these objects are affected by light. Look for sparkles, shiny surfaces, reflections, refraction, transparency, and translucency.

- Touch the objects and list as many words as you can to describe the textures and tactile feelings you notice. Use more than your hands for touching.

- Move the objects in as many ways as you can think of.

- Discover as many ways as you can to change, transform, or combine the objects (take things apart, stack, squish, pile, knock over, and so on).

- Notice what you are curious about and how you feel as you explore.

- Write a reflection of what you did to explore the objects and the new insights or discoveries you gained from this experience.

Observation Practice

As you read the following observations of children involved in sensory exploration, see if the Reawaking Your Senses practice enlivened your senses so that your observations take on new meaning and appreciation.

Bubble Symphony

As Shelby enters the room today, she is immediately drawn to the sensory table, which is filled with warm, sudsy water, clear containers, funnels, and a variety of lengths and diameters of clear plastic tubing. She touches the water tentatively with her fingertips and coos, "Ooh, warm," as she plunges her hands and arms up to the elbows. She gently swishes the water back and forth through the table, watching as the suds move on top of the small waves her motion creates. She

places a funnel into the top of a tube, fills a cup, pours the foamy mixture in, and watches as the water flows out.

"Look," she exclaims, pointing to the inside of the tube, "the bubbles are sticking."

Using her cup, Shelby intentionally scoops the suds off the top of the water and tries to pour the mixture into the tube. Some of it sticks to the top of the tube, while the

rest drips down the sides. Shelby puts her mouth to the tube and softly blows. The suds move toward the bottom, and a newly formed bubble appears at the end.

"Bubbles!" Shelby exclaims.

She sticks the end of the tube into the water and begins to blow gently, making a humming sound. She watches as the water jumps in response to her gentle breath, creating masses of cascading bubbles spilling over each other. Several children who have been working near her at the table follow her lead and begin to blow bubbles in the water and hum as they work. For several minutes they follow each other's lilting "oohing" sounds and rhythms. As they work in unison, their music is soothing and calming, a magical Bubble Symphony!

—DEB, EARLY CHILDHOOD TEACHER

Reflect on your own or talk with a partner or small group about your reactions to this story.

1   What do you think the essence of the water and bubble experience was from these children's perspectives?

2   What can you tell about what they understand and know how to do?

3   What do they seem to be exploring, experimenting with, or trying to figure out?

4   Describe an example of when you have observed children involved in this kind of sensory experience.

What do you focus on when you watch children involved in scenes like these? Do you think about the spread of germs, the mess, or the noise? What do you see as the value of sensory play? Do you see the learning that is taking place as the children work with math concepts, science and physics, small-motor skills, social skills, and cooperation?

Of course, identifying the learning that occurs in sensory play is a useful consideration. But more important, do you see these joyful moments of childhood and value the delight, wonder, and magic they hold for children? Do you see the rich detail of the children's involvement with the water in the Bubble Symphony? In this small moment, these children had the wonderful experience of sharing each other's way of being in the world. They were soothed and connected through their senses in the following ways:

- the sounds of humming together

- the smell of the clean, soapy water

- the feel of the warm, moving liquid on their hands and arms

- the sight of the waves rolling and sloshing; a flat, smooth surface; then dripping and blowing and a lively jumping design of drops and foam, water and bubbles

In the real world of early childhood programs, children's sensory exploration can be exasperating and overwhelming to teachers. A child dumps a container of water on the floor to watch the puddles form. Another paints all over himself because it feels good, and it's the third time today you've had to help a child change into dry clothes. At times like these, you may not be able to appreciate the magic and wonder of such moments. If you adopt the general practice of observing closely with awareness, however, you will generally feel calmer and more nurturing as a teacher. This careful attention helps you mediate any frustration you might have, and you will thus choose a response that supports the children's self-esteem and natural curiosity.

When you replace your frustration and your teacher to-do list and imagine instead the feelings that arise as the children engage in this shared magical world, you take on new perspectives. Maybe they are filled with awe, joy, closeness, satisfaction, or curiosity. More than just a simple curriculum activity that you planned, perhaps this experience calls on the children's amazing sensory capacity to be *in* the world. Read the next observation with these ideas in mind.

The Dandelion

Lara notices a burst of yellow hiding among the blades of grass. She squats down close to her discovery and carefully extends her finger. Slowly, slowly, Lara moves her hand closer to the dandelion. Touch. Lara caresses the golden surface of the flower, paying close attention as the tiny petals spring back in response to her touch. Her touch is so gentle that the flower itself does not even bend or sway. Lara stays with her flower for some time, exploring the petals fully as she moves her fingers around the edges and across the surface of the flower in all directions. A few minutes pass, and Lara leaves her treasured flower and proceeds to walk around the perimeter of the play yard. She stops briefly to examine another dandelion—this one is still closed—and then returns to her original flower. Lara immediately resumes her exploration of the flower, once again extending her finger to caress the petals.

—SHELLY, TODDLER TEACHER

Reflect on your own or work with a partner or in a small group to discuss your reactions to this story. Use the following questions to guide your reflections.

1   How would you describe the essence of the experience for Lara?

2   What do you think she is trying to figure out as she explores the dandelion in this way?

3   As her teacher, how would you respond? Why?

What is Lara's point of view in this story? Do you see this as a moment of wonder as she studies the dandelion so carefully? What wonders might Lara see in a dandelion? How does her deep engagement give you insight into her understanding about the world she is pursuing? When we watch Lara's actions closely, we see that they are practical as well as full of wonder. She is a skilled scientist, able to observe closely and try out her questions and hypotheses when she touches the flower so carefully. We have to take her work seriously because of the time and intensity she brings to it. If we stop and see it as she does, we are reminded of the complexity of a dandelion and the learning and enjoyment that come from deep investigation.

Immersed in the Pleasures of Paper

Amia sat up, looking eagerly with her big, bright eyes at the large pile of shredded paper offered to her today. She didn't jump in to explore right away; instead, she waited for teacher Dana to join in with her. Amia studied the paper closely, examining it and pulling it apart. Amia and Dana played with the paper in many ways—pulling the shredded paper apart, throwing it up in the air and watching it float down and fall gently on their faces. They also discovered it made a rustling noise as they shook it. Amia loved playing a game with Dana in which Dana would shake the paper, and then Amia would shake it again. Her face and eyes lit up brightly and her little legs moved as if she were dancing with the paper. At one point Amia put the paper up to her face and Dana followed her lead. They hid together under the pile of paper, peeking out and laughing joyfully.

—Shannon, Nicky, Maria, Dana, Kim, Cheryl, Cindy, Frances, Maria, and Angel, cohort teachers

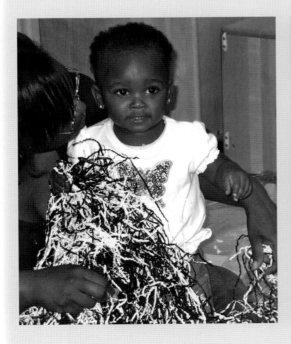

Work alone or with a partner or small group to think about this story, using the following questions.

1   What sensory element is Amia exploring in this story?

2   What do you imagine Amia may be experiencing and feeling in this moment?

3   How do Amia's interactions with Dana enhance this experience for both Amia and Dana?

Sensory engagement is an everyday occurrence for young children. When teachers notice the discreet details that children notice—the sound, light, color, and movement around them—and join in the experience, pleasure and participation are enhanced for both adults and children.

Take Another Look

Children immerse themselves in sensory experiences because these activities encompass action and interaction. Sensory experiences are soothing, freeing, and full of possibilities. Sensory materials feel magical to children when they manipulate and transform them. Children marvel at things adults find ordinary, messy, or even boring. From a child's point of view, there are so many new things to look at, hold, rub, taste, and smell. You need to record these details and embrace them so you can remind yourself and other adults about some of the most meaningful and vital experiences in the lives of young children. Here are more activities to enhance your ability to see and delight in these sensory endeavors.

Reflect on the Quote

Now that you've had the opportunity to awaken your own senses and to observe children's sensory play with a new awareness, consider these words of Buckminster Fuller.

If you want to do something good for a child . . . give him an environment where he can touch things as much as he wants.
—BUCKMINSTER FULLER

Discuss the quote with a partner or small group, and write down your reflections.

Read the following observation and think about how it reflects children's innate ways of exploring their world through their senses.

The Magic of a Sponge

Lorna offered her group of babies some dry sponges and tubs with a small amount of water in them. The children were immediately interested in this new material. They approached the hard, waterless sponges with great curiosity, and intense exploration began. They had serious looks on their faces as they examined the sponges closely while they were still dry and then quickly put them in the water. They manipulated the sponges, intently watching as the sponges absorbed the water. They also seemed inquisitive about the water when they observed their hands move through the water and made it ripple. The children discovered and then delighted in squeezing the water out of the sponges. They repeated the soaking and squeezing actions over
and over again.   —LORNA, INFANT TEACHER

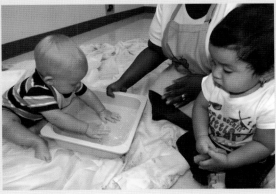

A simple offering of sponges and water led to deep investigation by these infants. They easily discovered how their actions had an impact on the sponges and the water. They seemed to learn from the materials, from their own actions, and from watching one another. We might say that these experiences relate to science and physics concepts, such as float and sink, absorption and displacement. These very young children's attention and ability to take in so much information so quickly are remarkable. They are just like the sponges, soaking everything up. Seeing the world through their eyes, we gain a new appreciation of just how amazing a simple sponge and some water can be.

Observe Sensory Exploration

If you approach observing with heightened awareness, you learn to see the smallest details of children's sensory explorations. This is clearly reflected in the observation of the babies with the sponges. Challenge yourself to notice children using their senses in the block area, in the drama area, at the painting easel, on a field trip, during circle time. Observe in a real setting with children or view a short video clip. As you observe, practice noticing the details of children's involvement, and then find the meaning by looking for the children's point of view. What seems to be the essence of their experience? What are they exploring, investigating, or trying to figure out? What do they find pleasurable, comforting, or intriguing?

Collect Descriptive Sensory Words

Because we are not accustomed to noticing details, our vocabulary for describing them is often limited. Here's a list of descriptive sensory words. Work alone or with others to brainstorm additional words to add to it. Keep this list handy and see if it helps you record the details and mood clues in your observations of children's sensory experiences.

Sense	Words
Sight	shiny, glistening, shimmering, sparkly, gleaming, glowing, brilliant, dim, hazy, foggy, transparent, glowing, silvery, flashing, colorful, vibrant, faded, vivid, pale
Sound	crunchy, crackly, sizzling, whirring, crashing, thumping, tinkling, whispering, yelling, soft, loud
Taste	salty, sweet, sour, spicy, oily, tart, bitter, savory
Smell	pungent, sweet, strong, musty, fresh, earthy, acidic, moldy
Touch	slimy, cold, icy, warm, cool, hot, prickly, soft, smooth, tingling, squishy, bumpy, gentle, rough, hard
Movement	glide, swoop, flutter, race, bubble, erupt, dodge, crash, bounce, speedy, graceful

More Things to Do

Here are more activities you can do to keep your senses alert and your awareness growing. You can do these activities on your own or with a partner.

Play with Bubbles

Gather a variety of bubble-making objects such as pipes, wands, strawberry baskets, and coat hangers bent into different shapes. Make yourself a batch of bubble solution, and spend at least thirty minutes blowing bubbles. Notice the shapes, sizes, colors, and rainbow reflections that your bubbles make. Try to make both really big bubbles and lots of very small bubbles. Chase and pop the bubbles you make.

Bubble Solution Recipe	
1 part dishwashing liquid (Joy or Dawn works best) 1 part corn syrup or glycerin 3 parts water Add dishwashing liquid and corn syrup or glycerin to water and mix gently until thoroughly combined.	

Use Your Nose

For an entire day, be aware of all the odors and scents around you. Go out of your way to smell flowers and take deep breaths of the air. Pay attention to the odors both indoors and outdoors: natural smells, human-made smells, pleasant and unpleasant odors. As you come across different odors, pay attention to how they make you feel and react. Write or talk to a partner about your experiences.

Jeweler's Loupes

Explore at least ten more objects with the jeweler's loupe, writing a description of the details and then sketching the objects.

Sample Observation Display

As you read the story below, notice how the teachers have incorporated the conventions of the New Zealand approach to writing Learning Stories. These stories contain the following elements:

- a detailed description of what happened
- an interpretation of what it means
- some teacher thoughts on opportunities and possibilities for what might come next
- an invitation to parents to add their ideas

The story is often written directly to the child, which helps the teacher to picture what she saw, what she knows about the child, what delighted and surprised her, and how the child might experience being told a story about this observation.

The Sea of Fabric

Nicolas, today I introduced some blue, sheer fabric, and it immediately caught your eye. You were the first toddler to jump right into the pile! You rolled in the fabric and held it close to your face. Did you notice the texture, or did you discover that you could see through the material?

Nicolas, you seemed so contented as you explored—you had a big smile on your face the whole time! You stood in the pile of fabric and slowly lifted it into the air. You allowed the fabric to drop from your hands and float back to the ground. After a few times, you tried to put the fabric over your head, but something seemed to be stopping you. Nicolas, you tried to bend forward to make the fabric fit over your head, but you did not notice at first that you were standing on the edge of the material. After a few tries, you realized this and stepped back. Suddenly the fabric was freed, and you were finally able to lift it over your head!

As you peeked through the fabric, you seemed so excited about your accomplishment! You continued to explore the material in many different ways—you jumped in it, rolled in it, and you covered your body with it. Nicolas, you even walked through it in different ways. You shuffled your feet through it and watched as the fabric gathered around your shoes, and then you took giant steps across the pile. Nicolas, you were so focused in this exploration!

What it means:

Nicolas showed us he is an independent thinker. He explored the material with his whole body. He was the leader in showing the other children that it was a safe place to play. He used many different strategies to explore the materials. Nicolas showed us the value of having adequate time to fully experiment with the properties of the materials, as he maintained consistent focus for the duration of the activity. We initially considered dimming the lights, but we rethought this idea prior to introducing the material, and it proved to be an important component in their investigations. Light allowed the children to see through the material, and it also allowed the children to see the shadows and layers in the fabric. Nicolas surprised us today with his flexibility to changes in the schedule and the addition of many new adults in the environment.

Seeking the parent's perspectives:

Dear Angela,

We would like to share Nicolas's exploration of fabric with you. He was so involved in the investigation! Please share your thoughts with us about this experience. Also, has Nicolas had similar investigations at home?

TEACHERS ELENA AND SHELLY

Mom Angela replies:

Rolling in blankets and pillows is one of Nicolas's favorite games at home. He asks his dad to play with him under the blanket on the floor. Also, Nicolas is very interested in textures. He loves to rub soft fabric on his face. His stuffed animal (Gomez) has long ears, and Nicolas falls asleep every night with Gomez's ears on his face. Even my husband's lens cloth for cleaning his glasses is something that Nicolas uses to rub on his face.

When Nicolas was still in my womb, we had a 3-D ultrasound, and the tech had a hard time showing us Nicolas's face because he had half of his face behind the placenta. I remember the tech telling us that he will love to cover his face, and she was right. That's the way he falls asleep every night!

Opportunities and possibilities:
Since Nicolas has an apparent love of different textures, we can offer him lots of texture variations in pillow coverings, beanbags, and textured storybook pictures. Nicolas might also be interested in using blankets to build forts and tents with his peers. We look forward to incorporating unique textures as part of our daily investigations with Nicolas!

TEACHERS ELENA AND SHELLY

Chapter 6

Study Session: Observing How Children Explore, Invent, and Construct

Play is the highest expression of human development in childhood, for it alone is the free expression of what is in a child's soul.
—FRIEDRICH FROEBEL

Learning Goals for This Study Session

In this study session, you will

- practice looking closely by making finder drawings
- examine the importance of children learning to invent with open-ended materials
- explore and invent with open-ended materials or loose parts
- practice seeing the details of how children use open-ended materials

Reflect on the Quote

Reflect on the quote from Friedrich Froebel that opens this chapter. Do some reflective writing about the quote or discuss it with others, using the following questions as a guide:

1 What do Froebel's words mean to you?
2 Do you have a story of seeing a child's soul while observing play?
3 Why do you think play is so important for human development?

Consider what this teacher wrote. How does it reflect Froebel's thoughts?

Children look at everything in an exciting new way. Think of how exciting our lives would be if we looked at life with this different perspective. My daughter (age five) and I were on the way to my class last week, and she was noticing the clouds as we drove. She noticed each one and how different they were from each other. We talked for twenty minutes about the clouds. Then she said, "When we meet Daddy, I can tell him how exciting the clouds are." I was into my busy day, rushing to make it to class, and she made me see the beauty I was missing. This quote, and especially my daughter, are great reminders of how nice it is to think like a child.—KARI, ECE STUDENT

Art of Awareness Activity

Drawing with a Finder

In Learning by Heart, Corita Kent and Jan Steward offer us another tool for looking closely. They created a finder tool from scrap material. This tool serves the same purpose as a camera lens or viewfinder. A *finder* helps take things out of context and allows you to practice seeing details without labels and judgments.

1. Create a finder for yourself. A quick way to do this is to use an empty 35-millimeter slide holder. You can also make your own finder by cutting a small rectangular hole (about 1 x 1½ inches) out of a heavy piece of paper or tagboard.

2. Take your finder with you on a walk around the building or outside, anyplace where there is a lot to see. Look at the world through the finder for at least ten minutes. You can do this alone, or better yet, do it with a partner and discuss what you are noticing. Remember, the goal is to practice seeing details out of the context of their name or purpose.

3. Next, use your finder to frame a small section of a picture in a magazine or calendar. Observe carefully what is framed by the small finder window.

4. Using colored pencils or fine markers, draw what you see inside the rectangle in an enlarged scale on an 8½-by-11-inch piece of paper. Changing the scale will cause you to notice the details in a new way.

5. Your drawing will be a larger version of what is inside the rectangle. Metaphorically, this is exactly what we are trying to do in highlighting our observations of childhood's ordinary moments, enabling those moments to become more visible to us and to the larger society.

Learn to See Childhood as a World of Possibilities

Children have few preconceived notions about what the world ought to be like, about how they should feel, or what they must do according to prescribed formulas. They view the world as being filled with possibilities. Each day is filled with the excitement of new discoveries rather than the pressing weight of obligations. Each minute and each activity is experienced as *now* rather than as a worried look into the future.

Unlike adults, young children have yet to develop permanent labels, automatic responses, or typical uses for most of the stuff they see all around them. They haven't learned the supposedly right answers or the right way to use things.

Sometimes this lack of experience and information can get them in trouble and put them in danger. Because of this, most adults see our role as protecting children from themselves. On the other hand, adults alternatively often see this innocence and ignorance as endearing and humorous. Children are viewed as cute, and we chuckle when kids say the darndest things.

When we watch children with openness and respect, we do not trivialize them in these ways. Close observation helps us see that childhood is filled with curiosity, creativity, and unlimited possibility. Children are born to dive in, take apart, rearrange, and invent, using whatever captures their imagination and curiosity, whether for a whim or an intense purpose. As grown-ups, we have a balancing act to do. We must offer the words and tools children need to move safely in the world *and* provide multiple opportunities and materials to expand their curiosity and inventiveness. We must focus on their curiosity and investigation as much as we emphasize their safety and security so we don't squelch their natural curiosity and their right to learn in their own effective ways.

The world of formal schooling and consumerism conspires against us in this work. The bulk of activities and materials made for and marketed to children are invented by someone other than the child. Parents and teachers think they are helping children by buying the latest fancy toy or curriculum package. Then they watch as the children become quickly bored and look for the next new toy or activity. All of us know the story of the child who plays longer with the gift box than with the toy inside. What children really deserve is an environment stocked with open-ended materials and loose parts, things from nature as well as the recycle bin. When we offer children these kinds of materials, they become creators of their experiences rather than consumers.

We adults are also caught up in this consumer world. We no longer see ourselves as creators. Commercial early childhood catalogs offer us prepackaged, prepared materials—things teachers previously invented for themselves. The following activity can help you remember the difference. It may be difficult and uncomfortable at first, because we are so used to looking outside ourselves for answers. Stick with the exercise to reclaim your own creativity and inventiveness.

Practice Exploring and Inventing with Loose Parts

Gather together a collection of open-ended materials both from the recycle bin and from nature. Some suggested items to have in your collection include the following:

- stones, shells, leaves, twigs, beach glass
- cardboard tubes and small boxes
- tiles, paint, and laminate samples
- yarn, wool, twist ties
- film canisters, plastic containers and lids, door hinges

Make sure you have many of each kind of item so there will be enough to explore and invent with. Work with a partner or small group so you can exchange ideas and reflections. Use the following guidelines to focus your attention and activity with the materials:

1   Explore the materials to discover how many ways you can sort and classify them, finding similarities as well as differences.

2   Next, use the materials to invent and construct something. You can do this alone or with others in your group. Draw on your explorations and discussions to inspire your invention.

When you have completed your inventions, use the following questions to reflect on your process.

1   Think back to when you first began to sort and classify the materials. What were your thoughts as you first started working with the materials? What strategies did you use to decide on the categories? What did you discover about this process?

2   Discuss the invention process. How did you come up with your ideas? What was your group process? What helped the group work together? What hindered the group process? If you chose to work alone, discuss why you made that choice and how it was different from the group work.

3   Think about the entire experience and how it relates to children's use of materials. What is the value of these kinds of materials? What do children gain when they are able to play in this way?

Try this activity more than once. Keep a collection of loose parts for yourself so you can turn to them often for sustaining your own creativity. Take this further by watching children and getting ideas from them about possibilities you never considered.

Following the children's lead can teach you a lot about flexible, inventive thinking. Here are some sample observations that bear out this point.

Building the Makeup Store

Today Dante goes to work creating something new in our block area. He first gets a clipboard, paper, and pen, along with a small Kapla block, to begin sketching out his plan. After getting part of his design down on paper, he stops to build what he has sketched; then he goes back to sketch the next step. This is repeated several times over a period of about thirty minutes. With the building of his design completed, he gathers mirrors and face paint from other parts of the room and announces to the class, "The makeup store is open. Come, girls, and get your makeup. Boys can wear makeup too."

—VICKY, PRESCHOOL TEACHER

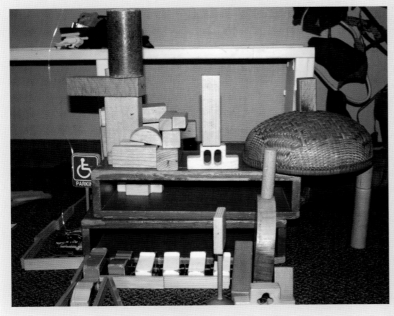

Getting to 100

Today the children were very inventive in trying to make the needle on our scale reach 100. Jonah spearheaded the exploration by bringing different things to put on the scale. As more children got involved, they began to discuss how the number was getting big enough. So more and more objects were brought and more inventions tried with their bodies.

— BETSY, PRESCHOOL TEACHER

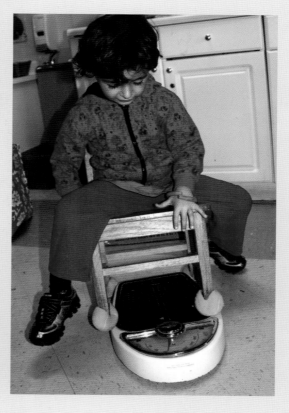

Ramps and Tubes

Lindsay decides to offer some new materials to her group today. She gathers together different lengths and varieties of tubes and wooden planks. She also includes some wooden spools and containers of small wooden beads and balls. When the children notice the new materials, they approach curiously but with caution. The exploration begins slowly. Austin carefully lines up two of the wooden planks using the small wooden bench to create ramps. Lee arrives and adds another plank at the end of one of the ramps and then adds one of the tubes as an additional ramp. As Austin watches, she begins to roll one of the wooden balls down the ramp.

Before long Austin and Lee have created a game, putting balls on the top of the ramp and exclaiming how fast they roll down.

"Mine's fastest! Mine's fastest!" Lee squeals with obvious delight on her grinning face.

The exploration and invention continues to unfold. Next, a group of the boys work together to line up the tubes from tallest to the smallest and begin to drop balls in each of them one by one.

Laughing excitedly, they knock the tubes over and the balls spill all over the rug. They exuberantly run to gather up the balls and begin filling the tubes again. Other children use the spools and tubes as telescopes, looking through them at objects around the room.

—DEB, TODDLER TEACHER

Reflect on your own or work with a partner or small group to discuss the meaning of these observations. Use the following questions to guide your thinking:

1 How did the children use the materials to represent something they already knew about?

2 What details did you notice about their use of the materials?

3 What new ideas did you get from watching their inventions?

When we look closely at these observation stories, we can begin to answer questions that lead us to more understanding. What roles do the environment and materials play in the children's play and learning? What happens when children are allowed to enter into play with their own interests and developmental levels? What is the value of children playing with the same materials over time? How does the children's play help them acquire social skills and develop relationships?

Beyond their learning value, open-ended materials offer children experiences with what is possible rather than what is *right*. When you watch, listen, and support children's inventions with open materials, you see their total focus and intense drive to make their ideas and hypotheses visible. You can watch the flexibility of their thinking as they figure out new ways to solve problems and accomplish their goals. You will see their delight in sharing and building on an idea with others. Watching children at work with open materials, you can understand how with time, opportunity, purpose, and passion human beings came to invent the wheel, build a community, compose a symphony, and fly to the moon.

Take Another Look

If you are working in a setting that hasn't previously made loose parts available to children, you will need to introduce them in a gradual way. Things like boxes from food packaging, paper towel tubes, and several rolls of masking tape make a good starting point. These are open-ended enough that children won't assume that you have something specific in mind to do with them. You can try modeling by using self-talk while picking up different pieces, saying things like "This reminds me of . . ." or "If I wanted to make something that needed a long tube, I could use this." Once children begin to see that their ideas can be represented with the materials, they will begin to use them more freely.

Designate a specific area of the room for your recyclable loose parts. Some teachers refer to this shelf or storage bin as *the inventor's box* or *the creation station*. In their book *Beautiful Stuff! Learning with Found Materials*, authors Cathy Weisman Topal and Lella Gandini demonstrate how teachers and children created a classroom space as part of a long-term project that involved families in gathering materials and children in sorting, organizing, and arranging the materials in an inviting way.

Offer Open-Ended Materials

Provide ample open-ended materials from both nature and the recycle bin, and watch how children use them. For preschool-age children and older, make sure you have enough items and materials they can use to attach things together—tape, twist ties, staplers, stickers, string, and wire. Make sure the items have no small parts or pieces that may be dangerous to infants and toddlers if you work with them.

Offer a selection of these materials every day for a week so you can see what happens over time. Observe attentively how the children use the materials, and reflect on the following questions, either alone or with a partner:

1   What do the children do with the objects and materials?

2   What seems to capture their interest?

3   What seems to be fun and pleasurable?

4   What experiences, people, and other materials do children seem to connect with these materials?

5   How do they talk about the materials?

6   How do they use the materials to represent their ideas, as symbols and props and as actual inventions and constructions of their ideas and play?

7   How does their use of the materials change over time?

Observe the Use of Found Materials

Make note of how children use open-ended materials they find on their own, either in the classroom or outside. Reflect on what you see, using the following questions:

1   What open-ended materials or items did they find?

2   How and where did they use the materials—for sensory exploration, for construction, for drama?

3   What do the items have in common?

4   How did the children use the materials to represent their ideas and understandings?

Reflect on the following story from Shelly about young Lara's interest in balance.

Experimenting with Balance

Lara travels around the play yard, stopping several times to examine little logs we've put around. After a few minutes, she chooses one log and carries it around until she picks up a second and then a third. Dropping them in a heap, Lara carefully begins to arrange the logs, laying them side by side, so close they are almost touching. She scans the area and quickly retrieves another log to add to her arrangement. Then she places her foot on the largest log, stretches out her arms, and moves her foot slightly. After a few adjustments, Lara lifts her other foot and places it on the surface of the log on the outside. She takes a moment to adjust her footing and then straightens her back and relaxes her arms by her sides with a giggle and a smile.

—SHELLY, TODDLER TEACHER

Offer Real Tools

With the obligation to keep children safe, many teachers have moved away from giving children real tools for building and construction. This is unfortunate, because children long to do meaningful work with real tools. What self-image do we leave them with when we deprive them of the opportunity to acquire the skill and safety precautions to use these tools for their work? With some thoughtful planning, children can learn to use carpentry tools (hammers, screwdrivers, saws, drills), craft tools (glue guns, carving tools), gardening tools (shovels, plows, hoes, pumps), and cooking utensils (blenders, citrus squeezers, cheese slicers, mortars and pestles).

Observe the Use of Real Tools

Study each of the photos and discuss or do reflective writing, using the following questions.

1   What do you see in the children's faces, hands, and body language that conveys what this experience means from their point of view?

2   How do you think the teacher might have prepared the children for using these tools?

3   How might you incorporate the use of real tools in planning your environment and curriculum for children?

More Things to Do

The idea of creating things from found materials isn't limited to young children. In fact, as you read about how artists, architects, and inventors develop their works, they often make use of some of these ideas and materials.

Try More Finder Drawings

Find more images to look at with your finder. Complete at least ten more finder drawings.

Observe Artists' Work

Here is an engaging activity that will help you see more details and look with the critical eye of an artist.

Visit an art gallery or collect photos or greeting cards with reproductions of paintings, drawings, sculptures, or other art forms on them.

Work on your own or with a partner or small group, using the following questions to analyze the art together.

1   What do you think the artist wanted you to notice about this artwork? Why?

2   What part of the artwork interests you most? Why?

3   Examine the different ways the artist used line and shape. Use your finger to trace them. As you do this, notice how they change and where they lead to and from.

4   Describe the patterns, colors, textures, and objects in the artwork.

5   How would you describe the mood of the artwork?

Learn to Use a New Tool Yourself

As you consider the possibility of offering real tools to children, find a tool that you have little experience with and explore how you might learn to use it. What might this tool allow you to accomplish? What precautions do you want to take in using this tool? How might you break the learning process down into steps to be mastered?

Sample Observation Display

In Jill's observation story, notice how she gives the reader a sense of knowing the child well, describes her curiosity about what kept Finn working to get the blocks to balance, and shares a window into how she thinks about materials that will engage children's interests.

Balance Is Tricky

Here are a few things I know about Finn: he likes to play with cars and read books, he likes his Legos, and he really likes to move. Another thing I've noticed is that sometimes, when the moment is just right or the classroom setup sparks his imagination just so, he will focus intently on something, no matter what might be happening around him. This happened one day recently.

Finn noticed our new set of rainbow blocks winding its way around the platform. After a few minutes of looking at the blocks, he brought over these wooden, boulder-type blocks that we have and got to work. He worked on balancing these blocks on top of the spiral staircase for about ten minutes. It seemed Finn wanted to balance all nine of the boulder blocks on top of each other, a tricky enough feat when they are on solid ground, but he was using the top of the staircase as his starting point. Each time some of the blocks fell over, he would start again with a calm and determined look on his face. It was as if he knew that his experiment was tricky and that the blocks falling were all a part of the process. Maybe the trickiness was what made it so satisfying for Finn?

The materials we choose to make available in our room have a lot of thought and intention behind them. One thing I like about teaching here is that we are encouraged to use natural materials in our classrooms. I think that it's important to make things look inviting and interesting to kids. As a teacher, I am constantly searching for new and unusual props and toys, always looking for new things to put together. I like that no matter how much thought I put into something, a kid will usually come up with something totally new and inventive to do with the materials. It does keep things interesting! I wonder what it was that made Finn think to put these two materials together, and what it was that kept him at it for so long. I plan to show him the pictures of his play and tell him what I saw and see if he has anything to add.

I like the idea that we have space in our classroom for both individual and group play. It was cool to see Finn so focused and uninterrupted in the midst of our busy room. I would like to continue to challenge Finn this year, to get him away from his Lego comfort zone a little bit more, and get him to share his ideas with others. I'll let you know how it goes!   —JILL, TEACHER

Chapter 7

Study Session: Observing How Children Connect with the Natural World

As a child, one has that magical capacity to move among the many eras of the earth; to see the land as an animal does; to experience the sky from the perspective of a flower or a bee; to feel the earth quiver and breathe beneath us; to know a hundred different smells of mud and listen unselfconsciously to the soughing of the trees.

—VALERIE ANDREWS

Learning Goals for This Study Session

In this study session you will

- reconnect with the wonders of the natural world
- learn to appreciate children's deep fascination and connection with nature and living things
- practice seeing the details of children's connections with the natural world

Reflect on the Quote

Think over Valerie Andrews's words, using the following questions as a guide:

1   What is your reaction to the quote by Andrews?

2   Do you have any childhood memories of seeing the world in the way she describes?

3   Have you seen children engaged with the natural world in this way?

Do some reflective writing and talk with another person or a group about your thinking. You might want to use these educators' responses to spark or extend your thinking.

There is such an incredible purity when a child explores nature. Much of my own childhood was spent with nature as my close companion. Babbling brooks and willow trees became like a second home to me. Sometimes I really miss those moments from my youth, the times in nature when nothing was expected or demanded and for just a moment, I could truly live. Now, as an educator of toddlers, I have the great privilege of witnessing these young children fall in love with the earth. There is something so pristine about a child's first experiences in nature that it beckons me to reunite with nature myself.—SHELLY, TODDLER TEACHER

My initial reaction to this quote is that of awe and sadness. I feel awe at the magical capacity children have to see the world as only they can, to see the incredible beauty in a snowflake or a grain of sand, to be able to smell the rain before it comes. I feel sadness because I think somewhere along the way we lose this magical capacity. And I wonder why that is or when it happens. I remember the long days I would spend as a child in the woods behind my house, the smell of the soil as it got darker as I dug into it, the idea that fairies really did live under the puff mushrooms and that the clouds were animals. I see this in children all the time when they are given the opportunity to really engage in the natural world.—LORRIE, ADMINISTRATOR

Art of Awareness Activity

Observing Nature:

Try this activity adapted from Corita Kent and Jan Steward's book *Learning by Heart*.

1   Choose something from nature to observe: a tree, a flower, the moon, a shadow, or a living creature, such as an insect or bird, your dog or your cat. Make sure you choose something that you can observe more than once.

2   Use the following guidelines to focus your observation:

 •   Look at the shape and the parts that make up the whole of your subject.

- Look for patterns and textures in the subject.

- Look for dark and light shades.

- Look for colors in the subject, subtle as well as vivid.

- Look for the different ways the subject moves.

3   Observe your subject for at least fifteen minutes a day for a week. Write a list of the specific details you notice each day. If you like, you can make sketches to go with your notes.

4   Keep an ongoing collection of the details of your observations. Notice the differences in your observations and in yourself each time you observe.

5   At the end of the week, get together with a partner or small group. Discuss the process you went through to study your subject. Share your discoveries about your subject and yourself.

Learn to See Childhood as a World of Natural Wonders

That was the main thing about kids then: we spent an awful lot of time doing nothing. . . . All of us, for a long time, spent a long time picking wildflowers. Catching tadpoles. Looking for arrowheads. Getting our feet wet. Playing with mud. And sand. And water. You understand, not doing anything. What there was to do with sand was let it run through your fingers. What there was to do with mud was pat it, and thrust it, lift it, and throw it down. . . . My world as a kid was full of things that grown-ups didn't care about.

—ROBERT PAUL SMITH

This quote from Robert Paul Smith illuminates the way we human beings have an ardent desire for places that help us feel connected to the earth and the sky and other living creatures. For it is in these places that we feel a part of something bigger than ourselves. Being outdoors is among the deepest, most passionate joys of childhood. There is the vastness of the sky and the intricacies of a leaf. In cities, the light bounces off buildings and creates shadows and reflections that are interesting to follow.

The outdoors has blustery, windy days that stir our bodies and our imagination. It has gentle rain that glistens and makes puddles perfect for jumping and splashing. The sun warms our bodies and lightens our spirits. The outdoors is full of creatures that scamper, fly, and slither. It is always changing and renewing itself. It is ripe for us to investigate and transform and create miniature worlds and dramas.

Outdoors, children can be loud and boisterous or quiet and contemplative. They can experience the life cycle, anticipate the changes in the seasons, and observe and care for living things. They can discover the different ways people live and work and play. Outdoors, children can invent games, learn how to take care of themselves, and watch out for others. It is a place for spiritual connections and emotional and physical release.

Sadly, the majority of children growing up in early childhood programs have outdoor time limited by a daily schedule and the restrictions of a concrete playground with anchored, commercial play equipment that doesn't

bend in the wind or change with the seasons. As the modern world gets bigger and fears about safety and liability grow, children have less and less opportunity to meet their critical human need for connection with nature. The dangers of this lack of connection with the natural world have been well documented in Richard Louv's work, including his books *Last Child in the Woods* and *The Nature Principle*. The good news is there are many local, national, and international initiatives designed to promote nature education and keep children connected to the natural world, including the Children and Nature Network (www.childrenandnature.org), the Nature Action Collaborative for Children through the World Forum Foundation (www.worldforumfoundation.org), and the Arbor Day Foundation Nature Explore program (www .arborday.org/explore). These resources help us remember the vital importance of protecting children's innate kinship with nature.

It is essential for adults who work in early childhood programs to recognize the profound importance of children making connections with the natural world. Observing children involved in these experiences is a way to inform and illuminate your own relationship with the natural world. Remembering your childhood experiences outdoors is another powerful tool for recognizing the significance of this with children.

Practice Remembering the Wonders of Nature

This activity will help you to continue to reconnect with the wonders of the natural world. Think about a place outdoors where you loved spending time during your childhood. Draw a simple map of this place, noting these features on the map:

- things that were growing: trees, plants, grass, or gardens
- living creatures you found: animals, insects, reptiles, or birds
- forms and structures, both natural and human-made: water, rocks, stumps, hills, sheds, barns, porches, hideouts, water towers, or bridges

- places where you played, what you played, and the materials you played with

When you have completed your map, share it and the stories it evokes with a partner or a small group. Compare the similarities and differences of one another's experiences. Discuss the value and importance that these experiences have played in your life. Compare your experiences to those of the children you work with.

Observation Practice

Remembering your own experience and those you heard about in the discussion, consider the following observations of how children connect with the natural world. A set of questions to reflect on follows each.

First Frost

It was a brisk, icy morning when the children burst onto the play yard bundled in coats, hats, and mittens. As they headed through the gate, they suddenly stopped, noticing the sparkly frost glazing every surface of the yard: the puddles, grass, tire climber, sandbox, and swings. Everything was coated with a thin layer of twinkling white ice. Children started running to all parts of the yard, testing the surfaces, shouting out to each other excitedly as they explored the enchanting landscape.

"Whoa . . . look!" Rebecca sang out as she approached the tire climber. She gingerly touched the surface with her mittened finger. When she lifted her finger and looked, again she said, "Whoa!" marveling at the impression her finger left in the frost.

She picked one of the last fall leaves, carefully investigating the tiny crystals on the surface. Then she gathered up a collection of the leaves, examining each one and lining them up along the edge of the sandbox. Next, she began rubbing and scraping the frosty layer off the wooden edge. At one point, Rebecca slowly lowered her head to the edge, stuck out her tongue, and licked the frost. She looked up with a beaming smile and exclaimed, "It's cold!"

Rebecca jumped up and ran to join the other children, who were stomping exuberantly through the grass, stopping and noticing each footprint they made with their movements. They followed each other's footprint trails, turning their wintry dance into a game of chase as the magical blanket of frost melted under them.

—Nancy, family child care provider

Reflect on your own or with a partner or small group to find the meaning in this story. Use the following questions to guide your thinking and discussions:

1   What do the children seem most interested in as they explore the frost?

2   What strategies do they use to explore?

3   What questions or hypotheses can you see them pursuing in the details of their actions?

When you watch children closely, you will see their quest to connect to nature. It's heartening to discover that when given the least bit of opportunity, children find the natural world in their environment. They discover the crack in a sidewalk and chip away to uncover the pliable dirt. They are drawn to every puddle in the asphalt streets of urban environments. Or, as in the "First Frost" story, they see magic and opportunity for discovery in the change of nature they experience around them. We must seize the opportunity to strengthen children's natural inclination to wonder and delight in the natural world. In her book *The Sense of Wonder*, Rachel Carson offers us a powerful vision for children and for ourselves:

> A child's world is fresh and new and beautiful. . . . It is our misfortune that for most of us that clear-eyed vision, that true instinct for what is beautiful and awe-inspiring, is dimmed and even lost before we reach adulthood. If I had influence with the good fairy who is supposed to preside over the christening of all children, I should ask that her gift to each child in the world would be a sense of wonder so indestructible that it would last throughout life, as an unfailing antidote against the boredom and disenchantment of later years, the sterile preoccupation with things that are artificial, the alienation from the sources of our strength (54).

There Is Something to See Over Here!

Jackson was playing in the sandbox when he ran up to his teacher, wide-eyed and with a huge grin on his face, and eagerly exclaimed, "Come over here! There is something to see over here!"

Teacher Jess followed him to the other side of the sandbox, where Jackson pointed out a big, beautiful butterfly. Soon other children who were interested in his discovery surrounded him. Jackson knelt over the butterfly and cupped his hands around it.

"Don't touch him," he whispered reverently.

Soon, however, he extended a finger and touched the butterfly. The touch was gentle, but he spoke eagerly, "I want to *catch* him, and I want to put him in a box and he can come *home* with me!"

Slowly, the butterfly fluttered across the yard, making frequent stops. Jackson followed close behind, with a look of wonder on his face. Although he continued to express his desire to catch and to hold the butterfly—in an increasingly assertive tone—he made only very gentle contact and made sure that none of the other children came *too* close.

As the butterfly flew over the fence and out of the yard, Jackson waved, calling out, "Good-bye, butterfly! Come back soon!"

—JESS, EARLY CHILDHOOD TEACHER

Keep these questions in mind as you review the story of Jackson:

1   What does this story show about this experience from Jackson's point of view?

2   What does it show us Jackson understands about the natural world?

3   Can you spot the skills Jackson is demonstrating in the story?

Jackson's story gives us a glimpse into children's inherent rapport and desire to be connected with the natural world. There was a surprising contrast between Jackson's emphatic words and his light touch and gentle behavior with the butterfly. He seemed to be experiencing an internal struggle. He really wanted to have a relationship with the butterfly by holding it and taking it home with him, but he also understood the fragility of the butterfly's body and the need to respect this living creature. The story demonstrates Jackson's growing understanding about the needs of other living things as well as his curious disposition and skills for investigating the world around him.

A Trip to the Woods

It is our second trip to the woods with our toddlers. As we creep through the overgrown jungle of branches and vines, two-and-a-half-year-old Liam stops in his tracks, his eyes wide. It seems that he remembers the tree from our first visit. Liam runs over to the tree and, clutching at its rain-soaked bark, he attempts to hoist himself up into it. However, Liam soon slips and falls to the ground. Just as quickly as he fell, Liam jumps to his feet and examines the palms of his hands before brushing them off on his pants. He stares at the tree and looks to be planning his next course of action. Liam's attention is drawn to some young green shoots protruding from the tree. He grips the young shoots firmly in both hands and gives them a quick yet forceful tug. Once again, Liam begins to climb. He puts one foot onto the trunk and begins to pull himself up, using the tree shoots as leverage. He confidently raises his second foot onto the tree trunk and, using his hands, he hoists himself up onto the landing. Liam turns, beaming with pride. "I did it! I did it myself!"

—SHELLY, TODDLER TEACHER

Use the following questions to help you reflect on this story about Liam climbing the tree:

1   What is your response to Liam's actions, and what might you do in this situation?

2   What is the essence of this experience for Liam?

3   What skills and knowledge does Liam show he has?

The treasures in the natural world are plentiful and provide many opportunities for children's learning and enjoyment. The outdoors provides open space and natural and human-made formations that invite jumping, climbing, running, and other challenging physical adventures. Sometimes they involve risk. Liam certainly shows his determination to master the task of climbing the tree. It might be our first instinct to stop this two-and-a-half-year-old from this behavior, which could be risky. But as we observe closely and see the details of his actions, we come to understand Liam's competence and the importance of this opportunity for his development.

Children deserve and benefit from the challenges and adventures that the natural world provides. Their self-esteem grows along with their physical and mental abilities as they negotiate risks appropriate to their personality and level of development. We want to keep children safe, but it is just as important for us to carefully study these moments to see children's competence and joy as they negotiate risky situations on their own. The natural world is a vital place for this to occur.

Take Another Look

Children deserve a reliable refuge from the hard, sterile, fast-paced, hectic world of modern society, as well as institutional settings, urban environments, and commercial interests. It is their right and our utmost responsibility. Use the following activities to learn more about children in the natural world.

Observe Children in Natural Settings

Go to the beach, a park, the woods, or other outdoor places where children are playing. Choose three different children to observe, each in a different age range. Notice the details of how they make connections with the natural world. Use the following questions to guide your observations for some written reflections or discussion with your partner or group:

1   What do you specifically see them do in relationship to the natural world?

2   What seems to capture their interests?

3   What seems to be fun and pleasurable?

4   What questions do they seem to pursue?

5   What are they trying to figure out about themselves and the natural world?

Observe Children with Animals

Notice the way children connect with the pets or animals in your program. Keep a small notepad next to the animal, and visit this location throughout the day when you see a child or children involved there. If you don't have a pet in your room, take your notepad outside with you each day and watch when children notice living creatures outdoors—birds, bugs, worms, squirrels, toads, and spiders. Take brief notes over a few weeks' time. Use the following questions to guide your observations, reflective writing, or discussion with your partner or group:

1   What do you specifically see them do in relationship to the animal?

2   What connections do they make with the animal?

3   What seems to capture their interests?

4   What seems to be fun and pleasurable?

5   What questions do they seem to pursue?

6   What are they trying to figure out about themselves and the creature?

More Things to Do

Besides watching children and their relationship with the natural world, it is important that you pursue a similar relationship. It will give you further insight into how to plan opportunities that encourage children's connections with the natural world. Examining your own experiences will lead to more meaningful responses to children's self-initiated explorations in nature.

Discover That No Two Things Are the Same

Working on your own or with a partner, find four sets of similar things from nature: two leaves from the same tree, two similar rocks, two of the same type of shell, or two apples or strawberries, for example. Look at each set for five minutes, and then list all of the ways they differ from each other.

Compose a "Dear Beautiful Butterfly" Letter

Write a dialogue between you and a favorite living creature, such as a bird, fish, dog, insect, lion, or butterfly. Think about what it would take to make friends with this creature. What would you have to do or say to be a part of its world? The goal of this activity is to challenge you to try out a perspective different from your own.

Try Another Perspective Just for a Day

Another way to try out a new perspective using animals is by exploring the children's book series Just for a Day. These books take readers on a journey from the point of view of various animals. For example, in *Catching the Wind*, the reader is taken on a journey from the perspective of a Canadian goose beating its powerful wings as it flies over fields and towns. In *Lizard in the Sun*, readers are encouraged to see the world from the point of view of a chameleon. Pick another creature and write your own version of Just for a Day with your insect's or animal's perspective.

Sample Observation Display

As you read the following Learning Story, notice the details of Dash's exploration that his teacher Jess makes visible. She is inspired by his investigation and curious about his family life. What better way to find out than sharing a story like this with Dash's family?

"In There! Those Leaves!"

Dash, since your first day at school, you have expressed interest in leaves. I have seen you collect them, rake them, throw them, fill your pockets with them, tear them, and share them with others.

Recently, I watched as you explored the garden. For a long time you stood just on the edge, looking at the plants. Then you glanced at me. Quietly, you asked, "In there? Those leaves?" You had such an intense look on your face! When I asked you what you saw, you smiled at me but didn't answer. Instead, you took a few steps into the garden and then crouched down so the plants surrounded you.

Soon you began to pick up leaves. You rolled them between your fingers, held them up to the light and peered closely at them, tried to push some back to the plants that they had fallen from, and smelled others. A few made their way into your pockets.

You were silent as you explored, even though other children stopped to ask you what you were doing. Occasionally your look of concentration was broken by a radiant smile. You continued your exploration by ducking down underneath the plants and then looking up. The undersides of the growing leaves seemed to fascinate you.

After several minutes, the bell rang for morning meeting. You eagerly climbed over the railing and joined the rest of your group at the studio door. As you went, you dropped several leaves, some pebbles, and bits of tan bark, leaving a trail behind you.

Dash, I am so glad that you have developed the confidence to explore independently at school. I so enjoyed observing your garden adventure. How rich an experience! I appreciate your attention to detail, your curious mind, and your intensity of focus. I wonder if you have experiences like this with your family. You seemed to be familiar with the way things grow, and you were surprisingly careful not to hurt the plants. It excites me to think that you might have been making connections between environments explored with your parents and our school environment. Our yard has so many more lush places to investigate. I am looking forward to your next discovery!

—JESS, EARLY CHILDHOOD TEACHER

Chapter 8

Study Session: Observing How Children Seek Power, Drama, and Adventure

There was a child went forth every day,
And the first object he looked upon, that object he became,
And that object became part of him for the day or a certain part of the day,
Or for many years or stretching cycles of years.
—WALT WHITMAN

Learning Goals for This Study Session

In this study session, you will

- reconnect with the exhilaration of feeling adventurous, powerful, dramatic, and competent

- examine the significance of power, adventure, drama, and risk for children's development

- practice seeing the details of children's play involving power, adventure, drama, and risk taking

Reflect on the Quote

Walt Whitman reminds us that children have a thirst for experimentation and almost literally take in what they encounter. What they see around them has a tremendous impact on their growing identity. Use these questions to spark your reflection on this topic.

1   What are your reactions to the idea Walt Whitman expresses in the poem?

2   What experiences from your own childhood confirm this?

3   Describe a specific example of how you see the children you work with being affected by what surrounds them.

Do some reflective writing, talk with a partner, or discuss the questions in a small group. You might want to use the teacher responses below to spark or extend your thinking.

I am always amazed at how children use dramatic play to act out everything. They act out daddies, mommies, and babies, kittens, bad guys, and superheroes. I think they are doing this to understand the world around them. They seem to have to become something to understand it. I think that's what Walt Whitman means by this quote.   —JOSIE, PRESCHOOL TEACHER

This quote really worries me. I see the children in my group, especially the boys, acting out all kinds of things they see in movies and on television. It is so violent. The latest rage is always the newest superhero movie. Even though we don't allow them to play with the toy guns or other weapons they bring to our program, they invent them. They call them lasers and spend a lot of time shooting each other and blowing things up. I worry that if what the quote says is true, then these children will become grown-ups who use violence to solve their problems.

—CARL, PRESCHOOL TEACHER

Art of Awareness Activity

Uncover Your Emotional Responses

As adults we've been taught to filter out and restrict the emotional responses we have to situations around us. Both cultural values and our personal dispositions have influenced the mind-sets we have developed about displaying our emotions. Children have a very different way of being in the world. Until they are schooled in another direction, their emotions are unrestrained. They don't stifle their reactions to experiences but rather give full expression to what and how they are feeling.

Children use pretend play and drama to understand and express the many feelings they experience. By taking on roles, they can explore other perspectives. To help you remember what this exploration involves, try the following activity.

1   Collect photos from a magazine, book, or website that depict people's faces showing a variety of emotions.

2   As you look at each photo, bring your emotional response to the forefront of your awareness. Try not to think about or analyze the photo; just let yourself feel your response.

3   As your feelings come to the surface, express them in a dramatic way. Use your body, facial expressions, and tone of voice. Express the feelings fully, with drama and flair.

4   If you do this alone, try looking in a mirror to see your own expressions. If you're working with a partner or small group, do it as a performance for each other.

5   Try this several times so you become more comfortable with feeling your emotions and acting them out. You will get new insights into how children are in the world—full of raw, uncensored emotions—as they try to find their place in the world.

Learn to See Childhood as a World of Exhilarating and Scary Adventures

Children are small and the world is so big. On the one hand, they are eager to explore and try everything. They climb, jump, and sometimes even try to fly. The sheer exuberance of being fully in your body is something many adults forget about and feel uncomfortable with. Too readily we try to tame children rather than share their sense of excitement. As they move about, children often pick up objects as props to reenact or invent role plays and dramas to express how they are coming to see the world. They explore how it feels to be a firefighter, princess, monster, or baby kitten. In doing so, they learn to see things from different points of view.

On the other hand, children are often beset with fears and hesitations. In the context of normal development, most children successfully wrestle with their fears and develop a sense of competency. Even when they have experienced childhood trauma, most children are resilient. With ample support, they can overcome an inclination toward fear, self-blame, or unhealthy coping mechanisms. The way adults respond to children's feelings, drama, and experiments with power has a strong influence on how children come to see themselves.

I Can Fly

Vinnie loves trying on the different outfits in our dress-up area. With each one he dons, Vinnie's face fills with fascination and a new adventure begins. Today he put on a costume with wings and immediately headed outside, skipping across the yard with his arms extended at his side and flapping in the air. As he approached the climber, he stopped for a moment, looking over his shoulder as if to confirm that his wings were still there. Then up the climber he went, and with a big leap, he launched himself in the air, squealing with delight.

—NANCY, FAMILY CHILD CARE PROVIDER

Vinnie and Kailee Rest with the Baby Dolls

The children frequent our yard swing for the gentle, soothing movement. Sometimes they chat and giggle with a friend, read a story, or share a book with me. They also use it for endless

scenarios of pretend play. Today Vinnie and Kailee carry their baby dolls on the bikes and move from blanket to blanket where little sea life creatures and other dress-up props await them. They stop at these blankets and talk about being underwater and then try out being the sea creatures themselves. Then on to the swing, where they show us it is clearly time for a rest after all that activity. Snuggling down and pretending to sleep with the baby dolls, Vinnie and Kailee squeeze their eyes tight in between peeks at each other and little giggles. This is so in character for Vinnie, who has an ever-expanding imagination. He is also a great storyteller, often talking about his sister. In real life, he doesn't have one, but he continually has stories about her.

—NANCY, FAMILY CHILD CARE PROVIDER

Observing individual children over time can reveal emerging patterns and insights into their preferred ways of playing. You can see their growing imaginations and competencies, and these provide opportunities for you to see how their minds work, how they form relationships, and how they take care of themselves and others. These observations also offer opportunities for deeper conversations with their families.

It's equally useful to observe an area of your play space, such as this yard swing, to discover all the ways the children use it. This will give you more insights into the children and ideas for further props you can add to their play.

Learn from Children's Role Plays and Pretend Dramas

A well-planned early childhood environment is always provisioned with miscellaneous objects and dress-up props so children can engage in little role plays and dramas. Traditionally, teachers have been schooled to set up a housekeeping area, but we know that children need far more than homemaking props to show us what they are learning about the world, to try out roles and different perspectives, and gain new vocabulary as they attach language to their actions. Offering a variety of open-ended materials as well as familiar objects will promote opportunities to engage in dramatic play. If you observe closely, you will see children creating little dramas in the block area, at snack, out on the play yard, and even with traditional materials such as playdough and puzzles. Putting culturally relevant props in your learning environment will allow you to learn more about how the children are coming to understand their world and identity. Adding gender-neutral as well as what is considered gender-specific clothing props offers additional possibilities into how children see themselves and what they are absorbing from the world around them.

I'm Superman!

The open-ended fabric pieces in our classroom are one of the many open-ended materials available to children every day. The kids often use them during pretend play for blankets, beds, picnics, and tea parties. This morning, Avery walked over to me with a clothespin in one hand and a sheer pink piece of fabric in her other hand, and said, "Put this on my head . . . like this." After we successfully secured the head piece, Avery walked over to get more fabric and returned with instructions on where

to wrap it and where to clip it, twice. After tweaking everything just right, Avery smiled and announced, "Superman!" I shared Avery's enthusiasm and watched her as she soared and twirled around the room with her declaration. In the very next moment though, my thoughts were running wild with curiosity about Avery's choice to describe herself as superman. I offered her another title for herself, calling out, "Super Girl!" and "Super Avery!" She replied with a smile and continued to proudly call out, "Superman!"

Avery created this vision of Superman for herself, and I love how it so boldly and definitively contradicts what Superman typically represents for young kids. This experience leaves me with some questions about Avery's intentions however. Is she familiar with Superman? Were her intentions to boldly go where no girl has gone before? Was she making a statement of her own? Is she creating her own sense of experiences and concepts of Superman?   —EMILY, TEACHER

Cup-a-Tea

The children found the china tea cups that we set outside as an invitation for play. Here's a conversation I overheard among two of the youngest.

Jonty: "Want a drink."

Imogen: "I get a drink."

Louis: "I get a drink of juice."

As more children got cups, a social situation developed, with children assisting one another to get their drinks ready. At first glance, one sees a child pour a pretend drink then hand it to another in sheer delight, watching as they "taste" what has been presented. Gabriel explains to us during the tea party, "I taste the lemon. My mumma got a cup-a-tea. I like some more, more cup-a-tea."

—MARIA, PRESCHOOL TEACHER

Maria works at a preschool in New Zealand, where tea time is a prominent feature of daily culture. Here's a reflection she wrote about the cup-a-tea observation.

I continue to learn more about this play. With the social roles involved, the pouring of drinks, the desire for independence, the imitation of the adult world and relationships, I am seeing the deeper learning behind this very familiar children's play. It was fascinating watching the children's movements and actions; I recognized many of the gestures used as being identical to adult gestures. They seemed to model our actions quite precisely, playing with the sugar sachets, looking at the paper or magazine, and making small conversation.

—MARIA, PRESCHOOL TEACHER

Scary Ninjas

As adults, we often wonder what effect violence seen in movies or heard in stories has on developing minds. Clearly the children involved in this game (Taylor, Miles, Ben, and Noah) have experienced narratives with "scary" or "bad" parts. The group directed me to a pile of tires set up in the sandbox and asked me to sit down. They explained that they were going to make a show, and that there were some parts that would be scary, but that it would be "just on the screen."

"We're going to be ninja heroes. Ninjas are sneaky bad guys, and they steal things," Ben explained. "Miles is a shy ninja who doesn't want to steal anything. Taylor is a princess. Noah and I are going to steal their stuff. We'll tell you if it's going to be scary."

The group began their show. Initially, Taylor and Miles had a group of three orange cones, which they did a brief dance around while Noah and Ben watched. Then Taylor and Miles walked away from the cones, remarking out loud that they hoped no one was going to steal them. Ben and Noah tiptoed over, grabbed the cones, and stomped away. While this happened, Miles and Taylor pretended not to notice.

Noah and Ben hid the cones in the Brown House (apparently their home), while Miles and Taylor "noticed" that they had been stolen.

"Oh no," groaned Miles. Then he looked at me. "This is going to be a bad part. But see, it's just a show."

Miles picked up a broom from the ground while Taylor hid behind a tree. "I am going to take care of the princess, and *I* am going to get our special stuff back!" he exclaimed.

As he waved the broom, Ben walked toward him. "I'm going to steal the broom because I am the bad guy. Then you fall down," Ben directed.

With some (feigned, I think) effort, Ben took the broom from Miles, and Miles dramatically fell to the ground. Miles lay on the ground for a few minutes while Ben brought the broom to the Brown House and hid it with the cones. He and Noah stood in the door and watched as Taylor rushed forward and pulled Miles up off the ground.

The two stood together quietly for a moment; then Taylor said, "This time the princess will help you with those ninjas, okay? This time the princess will help you fight."

Miles tried on a few muscle-man poses and made growling noises while Taylor danced around him. Noah and Ben watched for a moment.

Noah turned to me. "I think this might be a scary part again," he said.

"Yeah, yeah, that's okay," Ben added.

After a few more poses from Miles (and a song from Taylor!), the two pairs rushed toward each other. Miles pretended to fall down, and Noah held him on the ground.

"This is what ninjas do, so it's okay," Miles said to him. Noah (who in previous games had never had the upper hand in a situation like this) agreed. Eventually Taylor stepped in and began to pull on Noah's shirt.

"I'm going to help Miles now. I am going to pull you off," she said.

The game continued in this way for about ten more minutes. Ben and Noah stole things from Taylor and Miles, who pretended not to notice; Miles and Taylor tried to steal them back, usually with no luck; and intermittently there were scary parts, which I was always warned about ahead of time. After Ben and Noah had stolen every toy on the yard and hidden it in the Brown House, Miles declared that the show was over.

"Now, we take a bow!" Taylor exclaimed. Ben and Noah declined, but after Taylor explained to Miles that when a show ends, the actors bow, and showed him how to do it, he was happy to join her.

—JESS, EARLY CHILDHOOD TEACHER

Here is how Jess reflected on this observation:

After watching this show, I am more certain than ever that this group of children, who enjoy playing tough, are on their way to truly understanding the ramifications of such play. They are also developing creative alternatives that work for their peers *and* for their teachers. I am particularly excited by the fact that this has been accomplished in part by the understanding of the Crescent Park community that this kind of play is important. When we fully appreciate that young children are competent and capable individuals, we are able to guide them through meaningful dialogue and help them to accomplish big things.

We do not ban this sort of game at Crescent Park, because children who want to play in this way will find a way to do so. If we were to make an effort to enforce a rule against gun (or sword, etc.) games, children would develop subversive or secret ways to engage in this play, making it even more likely to hurt someone's feelings or body. If we are available to children playing these games, we are able to have meaningful conversations about the subject matter, perhaps allowing the game to become something more than a fight. —JESS, EARLY CHILDHOOD TEACHER

There are many real things to fear in the world, and our media culture often uses stories of violence for entertainment and commercial interests. Evidence indicates that this both appeals to and negatively affects children. Gaining a sense of power can easily become equated with violence. For young children, the distinction between violence with real consequences and the violence of a TV show or electronic game becomes blurred.

In fact, children's play often appears to have elements of TV shows, movies, cartoons, or video games. Children imitate the sounds of guns, bombs, and destruction and often lend their full bodies to a portrayal of explosions. This is understandably alarming to many adults. But rather than immediately responding with rules or other consequences, we need to do some research to uncover the emotional elements that make this play appealing to rather than frightening to children.

In his valuable book on superhero play, *Magic Capes, Amazing Powers*, Eric Hoffman (2004) describes the developmental underpinnings of children's strong attraction to superhero and weapons play. Hoffman suggests practical solutions to the dilemmas teachers and parents face with this play, as well as to the bias that is often embedded in it with the stereotypes so pervasive in our popular culture. When we observe closely and try to understand young children's perspective in this play, we can see it in the context of their social-emotional developmental themes. These include:

- acting powerful to overcome fears and feel competent
- trying out risks and challenges to develop self-regulation and an I-can-do-it disposition
- creating drama and adventure to try to understand the world around them
- representing what they've seen and heard from close observation of their surroundings or the media

In our adult lives, we may continue to work on our social-emotional themes by creating drama in our families and circle of friends. Or we may immerse ourselves in theater or literature to keep exploring these themes. Some of us find counseling or a spiritual group useful. Whatever our avenues to work on these issues as adults, we need to remember that children also need avenues for processing their emotions and evolving ideas. Recalling our own childhood experiences with drama and adventure will help us recognize this and remind us to provide those opportunities for the children in our programs. Your goal is to offer experiences for children to create and invent their own explorations of power rather than to consume and mimic what the media feeds them.

Practice Remembering Your Childhood Drama and Adventure

Recall some of your vivid childhood dramas and adventures. Use these questions to pull out the details of your memories.

1   Where did you play and act these out?

2   Who was involved?

3   What props did you use?

4   Where did your ideas for these experiences come from? Were they related to events in your family life or community or tied to things you heard about the world, books you read, or TV shows or movies you saw?

5   Try to recall the feelings you had when you acted out these themes. Did you feel frightened, helpless, competent, or powerful in your adventures?

Share your stories with a partner or small group, considering the following questions. If you're working alone, you might try writing about the topics suggested by the questions.

1   How were your experiences similar to or different from others around you? Was your experience more typical or unusual?

2   What value and importance did these experiences have in your life, both then and now?

3   How do your experiences compare with the experiences of children today?

As you consider the times you felt most powerful in your childhood, reflect on how often this was related to being daring and adventurous. Most of us have favorite childhood memories of play that the grown-ups would have stopped if they had known about it. Try to keep your experiences in mind as you read the following observation stories about children involved in drama, challenge, and adventure.

Bad Guys on the Playground

"Are the bad guys out there yet?" Nate excitedly calls out to Adam from the snack table. With this question, John, Lucinda, and Nate jump up to the window to look out at the playground with Adam.

"Yeah! There they are!" Lucinda declares.

The preschoolers hurriedly clean up their snack area and head outside. This same scene has been happening for a few weeks now. The preschoolers anticipate outdoor time with excitement and trepidation. The bad guys are three of the kindergarteners who join this group in the play yard for recess each day. They are bigger and older, and these three- and four-year-olds notice and respect these differences.

Once on the play yard, the chase game begins. Nate bravely runs up to the three boys and shouts and laughs, "You can't catch me."

The boys begin to chase him until he scampers to the top of the tunnel, the safe zone. His comrades are there waiting. The kindergartners keep an eye on them but respect the rules of the game.

John asks worriedly, "Did they get you?"

Nate says breathlessly, "No, I runned faster and I climbed so fast to here."

Lucinda brags, "Yeah, they can't get me too."

John says, "Come on, let's go! They'll never get us."

They run out to the center of the grassy area, taunting the bad guys, fiercely growling, with eyes bright and alert. The bad guys take the bait, and the chase begins again. The preschoolers' movements are quick as they dodge their pursuers. At one point, Adam runs to a teacher and clings to her side, hiding from Suki, the kindergartner on his tail.

The teacher asks him, "Are you done playing this chase game, Adam? You can tell Suki if you'd like to stop."

Adam looks out from behind the teacher, growls at Suki, darts to the tunnel, and bounds to the top. Safe again.

The game ends for today as the kindergartners are called back to their room. It will in all likelihood begin again tomorrow, as it has now for weeks and even years past. When the bad guys were preschoolers last year, they played similar games, only they called their foes the big kids.   —CINDY, TEACHER

Reflect on your own or work with a partner or group to find the meaning of this observation story. Use these observation questions to guide your thinking:

1   What do you think the preschool children are pursuing through this bad guy drama? What do they say about themselves and the bad guys that gives you clues to the meaning of this play for them?

2   What do their physical actions tell you about their abilities and the importance of this play to them?

3   In what ways are the kindergarten children playing differently than the preschoolers?

4   What do you think the kindergartners' point of view about this play might be?

5   What are the kindergartners gaining from this game?

In the bad guy game, each of the children seems clear about their roles and confident that they can handle the drama that unfolds. In fact, they seem to need this self-designed drama to reassure themselves that they are self-sufficient and able to handle adversity. What could be more important for young children facing a powerful, unpredictable world?

Notice how these children invented their own scripts for the familiar bad guys drama. They were drawing on internal resources, not acting out a part invented by Hollywood or an electronic game designer. This story shows preschoolers and kindergartners playing together. The opportunity to play outdoors in a mixed-age setting is good for both the younger and older children. The preschoolers shared these experiences:

- excitement in anticipating the bad guys and the chase; looking forward to it, even though they feel some anxious concern

- competence in their physical abilities, their abilities to run and climb

- willingness to continue the risk of going back to the chase

- certainty they can keep themselves safe with the rules, the safe zone, their teacher, and friends

There are fewer details of the kindergartners' perspective in this story, but we do learn that they played the same game when they were preschoolers. They obviously enjoyed it and can now continue playing from the vantage point of being older. The kindergartners shared these experiences:

- responsibility to take their role as big kids seriously, having seen it modeled the year before when they were preschoolers

- empathy for their preschool friends, with eagerness to challenge them to take up the exhilaration of the chase and find their power

- recognition that they are older and have worked through their fears

- experience of their own competence and abilities

In this drama the teacher's response could have been to take charge and try to stop the game. Instead, we see her understanding the excitement of feeling scared and powerful, while reassuring the children that she is watching the scene and looking out for them when she asks, "Are you done playing this chase game, Adam?" She pays close attention. If the game did erupt into a conflict that nobody wanted, she would step in. This is a tricky role for a teacher to play, one that requires knowledge of the individual children, group dynamics, and the meaning or rules of the game being played. Having mastered observation skills and knowledge of child development, you can stay tuned to the underlying meaning of action games and help them stay challenging while remaining fun and safe.

As you read in the last chapter, in years past kids got to play outside without constant grown-up supervision. They learned to work through these issues with each other. Though we can't leave children unsupervised in our programs today, we need to provide for and protect this kind of adventure play. If children don't get to experiment with power and adventure when they are young, they are likely to pursue more dangerous avenues in search of these experiences as adolescents.

Wind Dancer

The teachers in the preschool room offered cellophane paper for exploration during morning playtime. Initially Joshua was engrossed in exploring the paper for its sensory properties—how it moved and made sounds, and how he could see through it. It wasn't long before Joshua discovered that when he threw the paper in the air, it floated quickly to the floor. Joshua got up and began dancing around the room, throwing the paper in the air. A number of other children joined in. The teachers made a decision in that moment to bring the largest sheets of colored cellophane outside so Joshua and the other children could continue this exploration in a larger space. Their decision proved valuable, for the children were able to run and jump as they danced with the paper. The wind and sun enhanced the children's experience as they delighted in twirling with the paper, working with the wind to get the paper to fly around them, and noticing the colorful shadows the sun and paper made on their outdoor dance floor.   —DEBORAH, TEACHER

Think about the observation story you just read. Work by yourself or with a partner or in a small group, and use the following questions to guide you as you reflect on the meaning of this observation:

- What do Joshua's actions tell us about his discoveries?

- What seems most engaging to him?

- How would you describe his competencies?

When a child such as Joshua takes on the challenges of speed and coordination, he is both exhilarated and self-assured. As we watch his adventure, our adult urge might be to issue additional cautions, such as "Be careful" or "Slow down or you'll get hurt." We know it's our job to keep children safe. But wait; take another look. Joshua seems very coordinated and confident. Consider the benefits he gets from this pursuit as compared to reminders that he might get hurt. His teachers understand this when they move the activity outdoors where Joshua can truly immerse himself in this experience with the magical paper.

Our foremost job as teachers is to keep children safe, but safety should not be equated with the absence of any risk taking. What would happen if

Joshua could not pursue this challenge? How might he come to see himself and his abilities? How would he learn to self-regulate?

Self-regulation is the ability to consciously control behavior in a socially acceptable way. The ability of young children to self-regulate has been found to be a huge predictor of school success. In her book *Mind in the Making: The Seven Essential Life Skills Every Child Needs*, Ellen Galinsky (2010) reminds us that research shows the critical importance of children being able to initiate their own activities, sustain their play for extended periods of time, and learn to regulate their own bodies and minds.

Take Another Look

Think about these questions in relation to your interactions with children:

1 Do you keep an eye out for ways in which children can experiment with having power?

2 Do you listen and watch carefully and wait before intervening in play dramas involving power?

3 Do you keep your eyes and ears open for examples of how children view power, where it comes from, and what they can do with it?

When you watch attentively, you can learn so much more about this important aspect of childhood!

High Jumper

Today watching Caroline on the trampoline, we could see how powerful she felt in her body. She stepped up with an initial hesitancy, but once she felt the bounce in her step, her face transformed to utter exuberance. Holding on to the bar, Caroline knew she could keep herself safe. This was a special moment for us to witness as her teachers, because we more often see Caroline's cautious side. The trampoline must have given her the joy and confidence of being able to fly! It gave us an opportunity to see her self-regulation zone of proximal development and confirmed that this trampoline is a valuable part of our play equipment.

—Michael, teacher

Observe Children's Play Involving Power and Adventure

Spend some time observing children involved in an adventure or exploration of power. This could be happening anytime anywhere, indoors or outside. Notice the themes of the children's play and the props they use to act out their dramas. As you watch, ask yourself what might be influencing them. What are the underlying issues they are trying to work out through their play? Consider this example from a teacher in New Zealand watching a child at the easel.

Colors Are Power Colors!

Late in the afternoon, when most children had gone home, Alex spent forty-five minutes at the easel, painting and talking with me about what power looks like.

Emma [teacher]: What does power look like?

Alex: These colors are power colors. Power has a little drop of yellow and pink. I'll do lots of power. There's lots of little drops of power. Power has that [*Alex points to the white square she has painted*]. Power looks like that. Oma has power. I have power when I am at Daddy's.

Emma: How do you know when you have power?

Alex: I know because I can feel it. It feels just like dancing. I can show you on my painting. I'm getting the green and purple for power too.

Emma: Tell me about your painting.

Alex [turns toward me]: It's a long story. . . This is magical powers. It makes people turn into cats and dogs. All the dots are the river. The river makes power turn into something. I'm here. I'm showing everyone [the painting] and telling them where to go and then I turn them into things like a kitten. I got my power from . . . [*thinks for a little bit*] . . . nowhere. I just painted it. The green dots are a song. Yes. [*Alex sings, integrating Maori counting*], Din, do dee, doahhh! Dua, dora, wha! Iwa, tekau, tekau ma tahi, tekau ma rua, la du la . . . a cat, a dog. It's a song for the power. I'm done now.

—EMMA, TEACHER

Here are Emma's reflections on her experience with Alex.

There are a number of aspects of this experience and interaction that stirred me. This is not the first time I have sat to watch Alex paint. What I notice is that she always starts in the center of the paper and then builds her painting around it. It is as if she has this strong idea, and once she has positioned a symbol in the center, she feels the freedom to expand and grow her ideas from this central point. Alex takes charge at the easel, with her body language showing poise and strength. She controls the paintbrush with her hand, her eyes, and, I believe, her heart, all three working in collaboration to create and bring life to what she feels and sees in her mind and body.

Had I not sat and engaged with her about the meaning behind her abstract impressions, I would have missed out on the essence of her painting and the narrative that ran alongside what she was painting. Most likely, I may have only seen it for dots, lines, and splashing of colors.   —EMMA, TEACHER

Observe Children Negotiating Risk

Observe three different children on a playground or in another setting where they are able to challenge themselves physically. Ask yourself these questions to help you collect the details of how each child approaches risk taking.

1   What does each child seem to be trying to accomplish?

2   How would you assess their stage of self-regulation?

3   How would you describe this play from the child's perspective?

4   Are there any cultural influences you can identify?

Notice your own response to any risky or daring behavior the children try.

More Things to Do

As you strive to become more comfortable with children's risk taking and action dramas, you should also explore more of your own relationship to risk taking. Dispositions toward risk are different for each of us. Our own tolerance and safety thresholds need to be acknowledged.

Assess Your Own Response to Risk Taking

Look at the photos below and notice your immediate reaction. Are you alarmed, disturbed, fascinated, or delighted by what the children are doing?

If you were to place yourself on this continuum of possible responses, where would we find you?

- That's not safe! Someone's going to get hurt. I'm going to stop this right away.

- This looks really fun, but I can't allow the children to take this risk.

- I think I'm going to move in closer so I can be ready in case anyone needs help.

- Wow, I'm just amazed by how capable these children are. What new challenges can we offer them for safe risk taking?

Do some reflective writing or talk with others about the following questions:

1   What is influencing the first response you have to each of these scenes?

2   What specific details do you see in each picture to indicate children's competance in this activity?

3   What self-concept and identity are children developing for themselves in activities like these?

4   Are you satisfied with your initial reaction to this situation, or would you hope to respond in a different way?

5   As an observer of each of these play activities, what do you see as important to pay attention to?

Study Emotional Expressions

To continue heightening your awareness of the different ways adults and children express emotions, try this activity throughout the course of a day. Choose an adult and child to watch closely. Pretend you are their understudy, and prepare yourself to portray them in an upcoming drama. Pay close attention to their body language, facial expressions, tone of voice, and other ways they express ideas and feelings. If appropriate, take photographs or videos that you can study.

Practice standing in front of a mirror and portraying each of the people you studied. Do some reflective writing or discuss the details and discoveries of your day with a partner or small group.

Sample Observation Display

Margarita decided to make this observation into a display because she wanted to share this touching story of the children's physical and social competency and the caretaking aspects of their friendship. She wanted to offer a window into the value of children's perspective on risk taking and feeling powerful in their bodies.

Fast Friends

Tyler, Manuel, Francisco, and Jerry went right to the bikes today the minute we got outside. This is something they almost always do. After riding around the circle two or three times, making whirling, speeding sounds, they all rode to the fence, one by one and, without talking about it, got off their bikes and lined them up. I was so curious about this shared understanding they had. Did they make a plan ahead of time, or was this just a spontaneous, unspoken decision?

But then they got right back on again with Jerry taking the lead. Round and round they went, going faster and louder with each lap. I must confess I was getting a bit anxious about their speed when suddenly Jerry's bike tipped over and he fell forward. Before I could even get over there, Tyler called, "Stop, Stop!" He quickly got off his bike and went to help Jerry. Manuel and Francisco jumped off their bikes and hurried over. Tyler leaned down and began to lift Jerry up by the arm. "Get him! Get him! Help! Help! Help me get him!" Jerry pushed himself up the rest of the way, and the boys all headed back to their bikes, and the fun began all over again.

I restrained myself from issuing cautions to be careful. Surely this experience had taught them that, and they didn't need another reminder from me. I know that sometimes when children race their bikes, take risks, and make sounds, we adults have the urge to stop them. But I've learned to try to see what this must feel like for them. Children find all sorts of ways to explore what their bodies can do, how much power they have, and how to make friends with other children. It often looks different from what adults would like to see, but these physical activities help them grow in their confidence and skills.

Today I was especially impressed with how capable these boys were with each other, not only physically, but socially and emotionally. Tyler doesn't share the same first language as the other boys, but that never seemed to inhibit their ability to communicate with or understand each other. I'm so pleased to see these boys have become fast friends, enjoying the exhilaration of bike riding while staying alert and taking care of each other.   —MARGARITA, TEACHER

Chapter 9

Study Session: Observing Children's Eagerness for Drawing, Symbolic Representation, and Literacy

Every child has a story to tell, and within that story is the secret to reaching her or him as a learner. Children's stories are windows into their uniqueness and clues on how to connect the child and the curriculum.
—HERB KOHL

Learning Goals for This Study Session

In this study session, you will

- practice using a writing web to capture details that spark your creative thinking
- recall memories of your own "storytelling" as a child
- examine how children use materials to tell stories of what is on their minds
- practice observing the details of children's efforts to represent their experiences and understandings through verbal language, drawing, and representational work

Reflect on the Quote

Reflect on words Herb Kohl's words about children's stories. Use the following questions to guide your thinking:

1   What do you think Kohl means by saying that children have stories to tell?

2   How do you think this relates to observing children?

Do some reflective writing or discuss this with others. Consider this teacher's reflection along with your own.

As I've been learning to observe children, I am beginning to see that everything they do shows me the story about what they are thinking and feeling. I feel like I have really changed how I think about them. I used to think they were cute and fun to be with. Now I think of them as amazing, complicated people, full of curiosity and adventure. I guess you might say being with them is like reading a good book or story. I can't wait to see what will happen next.
—AIDA, PRESCHOOL TEACHER

Art of Awareness Activity

Write the Natural Way

In *Writing the Natural Way*, Gabriele Rico (2000) describes a creative writing process she designed by observing the natural writing and storytelling strategies of young children. Her observations of children led her to believe that children who bring an attitude of wonder and openness toward creative expression are eager to dictate and write elaborate stories at a young age. She states that the ways we are taught to read and write in school inhibit our natural urge for self-expression because of the emphasis on rules and standards. The techniques she details in her book are designed to release creative potential and to trigger language capabilities from the right hemisphere of the brain. They involve clustering and webbing activities to call on the creative storytelling side of the brain before trying to use rules and conventions of writing to construct a product.

Rico makes the case that these are two very distinct aspects of writing. When we are forced to focus only on the conventions of writing, we lose the joy and motivation of expressing ourselves in writing. Try this webbing activity adapted from her book to stretch your creativity and experience the natural source of pleasure and gratification that writing can offer you. It will also help you begin to notice the beauty in the details of what is around you all the time.

1   Choose something in nature that captures your attention, and make this the focus of your observation.

2   Draw a circle in the middle of a piece of paper. In the middle of the circle, write a word or phrase for what you are observing.

3   Look closely at the object or animal, noticing the sensory details—color, texture, light, sounds, how your body feels—and what is on your mind as you look.

4   Brainstorm words to describe the details you're noticing. Surround the circled word or phrase with new phrases or words, and connect them to the central ones with lines. Your paper will start to look like a spiderweb. Look at the following webs for an example. Think of as many descriptive words as you can, and add them to the web.

5   Use the words on this web to begin to formulate some sentences about your experience.

Here are some examples of how teachers have created webs and turned them into stories. Beginning with something alive in the natural world, rather than a child, is a good place to start. It frees you from the concern about getting it right.

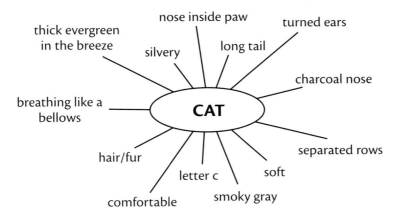

The smoky silver-gray cat is sleeping soundly, charcoal nose tucked neatly inside a tightly curled paw. Slow, rhythmic breathing gives the illusion that he's an old bellows fanning the blacksmith's hot coals. The curve of his back forms a perfect letter C that ends with the pointed tip of his long tail curled gently around his hind leg. His ears are tweaked clockwise to his head. His fur separates in rows of varying lengths as the bellows inside him fills with air and gently exhales. The uneven rows remind me of an evergreen tree blowing in the breeze. He looks very comfortable. I think I'll let him sleep.—KATHY

My son got out his high-powered telescope and focused it on the moon. It was the first time I had really seen the moon. The moon, whiter than the purest newly fallen snow, glistens, crystal cold in the clear, dark night sky. Mountains with jagged peaks appear. Close by, a huge crater lies, reminding me of the splash made by cereal when it is poured into white milk. Thousands of smaller craters cover the cold, milky white surface of the moon, making pockmarks.—GAIL, STUDENT TEACHER

Learn to See Childhood as a Time to Construct Meaning

When provided with open-ended materials, time, and support, young children eagerly create representations of their ideas and experiences. When you observe closely, you can see that these are more than creative outlets. Representational experiences are central to children's learning processes. They help children make meaning out of the social and cognitive code systems that shape their world.

Children are typically less inhibited than adults about openly playing with understandings as they build, take on pretend roles, draw, paint, and use any object within their reach to show what is on their minds. These initial expressions of symbolic thinking help children organize their understanding of the world and lay the foundation for working with other symbolic languages such as print, math concepts, and computer programming. These opportunities strengthen the parts of their brain that allow them to communicate in and interpret a wide range of representations, including written and spoken languages, music, dance, science, poetry, and literature.

In our efforts to get children *ready* for school, we often reduce or trivialize their opportunities for creative representation by giving them projects like making bunnies from paper plates. This limits their creativity and sense of possibility. Children gain experience in symbolic thinking and communicating through their creative representations. If the outcome of an art project is merely learning to follow directions or to copy a model, it will not reinforce children's symbolic thinking, which is crucial for early literacy.

A similar process occurs when we reduce learning to speak, read, and write to repetition, memorization, and copying letters. The sense of power and expansiveness that comes from mastering a language, from reading and writing, eludes children who are only taught through out-of-context, prescribed literacy activities. In contrast, children who are surrounded by meaningful vocabulary, print, art, and stories can't wait to unlock the secrets of this powerful form of human communication—written language.

When we carefully study their activities, both processes and products, we begin to discover children's unique expressiveness and their remarkable abilities to create form and structure out of the complex and often confusing world they live in. We see their eagerness to learn to use the tools and skills that will help them make their questions, thinking, and feelings visible. As Herb Kohl reminds us, when we watch closely we can see the amazing stories children are telling us about themselves and the sense they are making of what's around them.

Children's readiness to learn comes from their natural curiosity about the world and the urge to make sense of it through creative, investigative representations. Educators must overcome limited thinking about giving children craft projects as a curriculum for artistic expression. As the educators of Reggio Emilia have taught us, encounters with different art materials can offer children a hundred languages to think with and express themselves in. These media can build their brain's capacity for symbolic thinking. While verbal-linguistic skills and a rich vocabulary give children a solid foundation for literacy, we must also give attention to and respect the various forms of stories children bring to us.

Practice Remembering Your Own Storytelling

Think back to your own childhood and the way you used symbolic representation to express yourself and make sense of the world. Describe the forms you used and some specific details about what you did. Consider the categories of representation listed below as you search your memory bank.

- **Pretend play:** What open-ended props did you use? What were the themes and stories of your dramas?

- **Drawing or painting:** What tools and materials did you use? What do you remember trying to accomplish with your drawing or painting?

- **Constructing, sculpturing, designing:** What tools and materials did you use? What were you trying to express with these materials?

Reflecting on these memories, how do you think these experiences influenced how you see yourself as a thinker today? Do you think of yourself as eager to express your ideas with different materials? What artistic, musical, or literary expressions of others do you enjoy today?

How do you relate your own experiences to your work with children? It is also useful to remember specific experiences you had with learning to read or write.

1   What do you remember about how you learned to read and write?

2   What were the positive and negative aspects of the learning process?

3   Did you grow up thinking of reading and writing as strictly functional tasks, or did you seek out these activities as sources of pleasure in your life?

4   If your home language was not English, did you grow up with support for becoming fluent in both languages? How do you feel about being bilingual or about losing that opportunity as a result of your home life or schooling?

Observation Practice

As you study these four examples of children's representations, consider again Herb Kohl's idea that these represent children's stories about what they understand.

Representations of Children's Ideas

Erick, one of our children on the autism spectrum who rarely verbalizes anything, was captivated today at the flubber table. He patted the flubber into a circle and then tore off little pieces to put around the circle, surprising us all by saying "sun."

—Yvonne and
Megan, teachers

I've been working to promote positive social behaviors in our room by exploring the children's ideas of friendship. Today Melia made this drawing, explaining, "She's sad and her friend is bringing her flowers." I could clearly see the tears coming out of the sad child's eyes.

—Ann, teacher

Today in the block area a small group of children worked for almost an hour creating a house they wanted for our visitors. I was amazed at the time they took to tape together cardboard, search out fabric pieces, and use clothespins to represent the house design they had talked about.   —Briana, teacher

Caitlin came to preschool tentative about writing her name. In the last few months, we see her not only writing it with confidence but also using drawing and other materials to communicate her ideas, always adding her signature to each one.

—Sandra, teacher

As you consider the representations by these children, reflect on your own or with a partner or small group, using these questions to guide your reflections about each example.

1   What details do you notice about how the children used the materials?

2   What story do you think each child is offering with the representation?

3   What skills and knowledge does this work show us that each child has?

4   Is there anything in these representations that deepens your understandings about children as symbolic thinkers?

When you study each of these representations carefully, you not only notice the imaginative and skillful ways the children represented their ideas, but you also get a window into how each of the children is thinking. Erick, though a child with special needs, clearly associates his understanding of the sun with a circle, and he goes on to demonstrate his understandings of the rays of the sun or its brightness. Melia may not yet have demonstrated the kind of social skills her teacher is looking for, but she has clearly shown her teacher she knows that friends try to help sad friends feel better. The house builders have shown us that they understand that walls can be constructed out of different materials, that there are often peaks in a roof, and that fabric is often used in homes to add aesthetic elements. Caitlin shows us that she not only knows how to accurately write all the letters of her name, but that she understands that signatures identify who has written or created something. She has discovered that the spoken word can be written down and read aloud, an important understanding of the function of literacy.

An important task for early childhood teachers is helping children with language and literacy development. This can be easily integrated into supporting the development of their social skills. As you work to help children attach words to actions and ideas and to expand their vocabulary, you should not overlook the other forms of communication children are readily using. When you observe carefully and go beyond an interest in getting the children to use their words, you often discover previously unrecognized skills and understandings in the children. A rich supply of open-ended materials in your classroom will provide these opportunities for children to express what you may not yet know they comprehend or know how to do.

Ella's Puppet Stage

In recent days, Ella has been fully engaged with a space in our room that has acquired the name "the making table." Featuring a large wooden table, baskets filled with materials such as boxes and tubes, and shelves of jars filled with all different kinds of recycled treasures, tape, scissors, staplers, and glue, this space was designed for our children to express themselves creatively in many different ways. Each child who encounters this space seems to work in a different manner. Often complete spontaneity ensues, which we absolutely love, and in other moments, the children enter the space with a preconceived idea in mind.

In Ella's case, she knew exactly what her hopes were. She wanted to make a stage where puppets could tell stories of Ella's creation. Ella is a keen writer, and so it seemed important for her to first write a plan. She naturally sourced a pen and paper and asked for help to write that she wanted her stage to be pink and have white curtains on either side. She often referred back to this as she constructed her stage and was delighted with the end product. Upon completion of her stage, Ella went on to write out the steps she took to construct her stage. As Ella went on to create her puppets, we saw the same careful attention to detail, resourcefulness, and skill in accessing the tools she needed to represent the characters she wanted on stage.

—GEMMA, TEACHER

Read Gemma's reflections as she studied her documentation of Emma.

Emma was so proud of her writing and seemed to enjoy every minute of it, which I believe is due to the fact that she had complete ownership of what she was writing about. The source behind her writing was a real experience that she had an emotional attachment to, and therefore it was meaningful to her. This was heartening to us, as we work to ensure that literacy experiences are deeply connected to the children's interests at the time and are therefore relevant and meaningful.—GEMMA, TEACHER

Symbolic representation comes in many forms. Pretend play and drawing are a large part of the symbolic thinking that children use in early childhood. If they are surrounded with a print-rich environment where literacy is used in meaningful ways and is about real-life events and activities, then children come to understand print's power and purpose quickly. We can see this so clearly in the story of the puppet theater. Children are eager to know about and use the symbols that represent ideas and words. They show us this in all of the ways they pretend to write in their play and in their practice attempts at reading and writing.

Making Signs

Last week in our room we heard loud, strange sounds coming from the hallway. The kids were immediately curious and ready to find and figure out what the noises were. I took the group into the hallway to find some answers. We found large machinery and a few men in the community studio fixing something. We didn't know who they were or what they were fixing, though. Coming back to the classroom, Ainsley and Sarah gathered paper and pens and went straight to work.

Sarah: Hey Sandra, can we hang up signs on all the doors?
Teacher Sandra: What's this about?
Sarah: Of what we think is going on in the big studio.
Teacher Sandra: Sure. What do you think is going on?
Ainsley: Working on pipes!
Teacher Sandra: Working on pipes?
Sarah: Yeah. We think those guys are working on the pipes, and we want to tell the other kids in case they are worried.

I helped the girls get set up with thicker pens and paper. We counted the rooms (seven), and then I went through each letter for the sign *WORKING ON PIPES*.

They worked for a while, making sure each letter was correct, until Sarah looked up and said, "Oh man, how many more?"

Ainsley looked at me, and I suggested they count how many signs they had made.

Ainsley: One, two, three, four.
Teacher Sandra: You need seven. So how many are left?
Ainsley: Three more!

The two girls finished the signs and asked for me to take them around the center to hang them. They had made enough for each room and were very proud of themselves.

—SANDRA, TEACHER

Reflect on this story by yourself, with a partner, or with a small group. Use these questions to guide your reflections:

1   What motivated these girls to start making signs?

2   What made it possible for them to execute their plan?

3   What understandings and skills do you see these girls demonstrating in this observation?

4   Think of all the places you typically have reading and writing materials in your home. When children see all the places and ways in which reading and writing are useful, they will naturally want to express themselves in this way, as is so clearly evident in this story of sign making.

5   How can the many routines of reading and writing in the adult world be made more visible so the children can become involved in your program? For instance, are there clipboards readily available for the children's use?

6   Watch for examples of how children want to express themselves in writing when you model and narrate the purpose of print.

To observe children telling stories about their ideas, you will need to enrich your environment with representational materials. You can also set up routines for children as they play to encourage them to re-represent an idea in a different material. Designate clipboards and special pens as tools for thinking and representing their ideas. For instance, encourage them to draw a block structure they have created, to use clay to recreate something they have drawn, or to act out a story they have read or told. Make use of laptops and whiteboards for children to revisit their work and to add something new to their ideas to deepen their thinking. Once you initially model and coach children in re-representing their ideas, you will start to observe them initiating this routine on their own.

Take Another Look

If you watch for them, you will see children using representations in meaning-ful ways all the time. Try some of the following activities in your own setting to strengthen your commitment to provide these opportunities.

Examine and Enrich Your Environment to Support Literacy

Examine your learning environment, indoors and outdoors, to see where more open-ended materials can be provided for children to use symbolically in their play. Look for places where drawing, reading, and writing materials can be added to encourage children to play with creating and decod-ing symbols and literacy activities. Beyond a reading or writing corner, do you have books, drawing materials, and writing mate-rials in most areas of your room? Are they available for use outside? To encourage writ-ing, have a basket of

name cards and photos of each child as a resource for the children to write messages to each other. Set up a message center with a labeled mailbox for each child and a good supply of envelopes, paper, pencils, and pens. Next to where parents sign their children in and out each day, have a parallel sign-in area for the children to use. Depending on the age group of your children and your use of computers, scanners, and printers in the program, you might want an in-house e-mail system for them to send messages and drawings to each other as well.

Many early childhood resource books list props that can be put into the environment to encourage chil-dren to incorporate various forms of early literacy into their play. For instance, see our books *Designs for Living and Learning, Reflecting Children's Lives,* and *Learning Together with Young Children.* Help children use begin-ning reading, drawing, and writing in their daily activi-ties. In addition, you want to expose them to other ways adults use literacy for work routines—seeking out information online and in reference books—and enjoyment of reading, journal writing, and staying connected to family and friends who are not in their daily lives.

Observe Children Engaged in Using Language, Literacy, and Symbolic Thinking

Once you have the props in place, observe the children's use of them in their play. Each day as you watch children at play, you will see numerous examples of their expanding understandings of working with symbols, language, and literacy. Studying your own observations and the photos below, ask yourself these questions to deepen your insights into how children are communicating.

1   What details have you noticed about how the children are using the props?

2   How are the children exploring symbols, decoding or interpreting them, or symbolically representing ideas?

3   What do the children seem to understand about literacy and symbolic representation and how to use them?

4   What are the children's attitudes toward literacy? How can you tell?

5   Have you seen examples of children forming bilingual identities?

Examine Your Environment and Enrich It with Other Representational Materials

In addition to literacy materials, what other kinds of representational materials are available for children to use in exploring and expressing their ideas? Here are some questions to ask yourself as you assess your environment:

1   Does the dress-up or dramatic play area have props that are more open-ended than those for just the traditional housekeeping or topical themes like doctor's office and grocery store?

2   What more open-ended materials would allow for any of these themes to be represented by the children as they create their own props?

3   What kinds of open-ended building and construction materials are available?

4   Have you enriched the traditional supply of blocks and Legos in your learning center with things such as different-sized rocks, driftwood, sturdy cardboard tubes, ramps, gutters, carpet and fabric scraps, masking tape on dispensers, and sign-making materials?

5   Are there numerous materials available like glue, tape, and wire for children to attach things together?

6   Are there clipboards and thinking pens readily available to the children (for instance, extra-fine black markers next to clipboards rather than the thick colored ones typically used in the art area)?

7   Is there an art area or studio with a variety of everyday representational materials available? Have you coached children in how to use them effectively?

Study Children's Work

Along with your own observation examples, study the following examples of children's eagerness to represent their ideas symbolically with different materials. Use the following questions to guide your study.

1   What details do you notice about how children expressed their ideas?

2   Are there any new thoughts these representations give you about the children's ways of thinking and expressing themselves?

3   What additional materials would you like to introduce to your children so they can demonstrate their ideas with other media?

Sample Observations

Emma spent a long time creating a drawing with a story about the North Star. Because she seemed so deeply engaged, we offered her the opportunity to re-represent her star out of clay. She seemed even more intently focused than when she did her drawing.

—BETSY, TEACHER

Making birthday cakes has been popular in our toddler room these past few weeks. This morning Myla made an enormous cake with our classroom blanket. The colored water bottles and metal goblets became the carefully placed candles. Myla even walked around to each individual candle, taking care to light each one using a playdough tool as the lighting apparatus.   —EMILY, TEACHER

Victor has continued to revisit his earlier theories about how the water moves through pipes. Today he used the laptop to revisit how he had transferred his ideas from a two-dimensional drawing into a clay representation. As he started to make a drawing, he said, "This is what I drew then; this is what I know now."

—FRAN, TEACHER

Study Self-Portraits and Name Writing

Literacy specialist Evelyn Jackson Lieberman suggests that preschool teachers periodically ask children to draw a picture of themselves and write their names from the very beginning of their time in your program. For their self-portrait work, you can alternately offer children mirrors and photographs of their faces. Coach them in looking at details. For example, ask, "Do you see where you have hair around your eyes? We call the hair above your eyes *eyebrows* and the hair attached to your eyelids *eyelashes*." "Do you know where the top of your nose is compared to your eyes?" Use different drawing and painting tools for each child's self-portrait. Thin black markers on white paper will make the details stand out more. Eventually you may want to add color and different sizes of markers or brushes to more accurately capture the details of what the children are seeing. Learning this visual discrimination will help children in all their literacy efforts.

If the children say they don't know how to write or spell, suggest that they just pretend to write their name. Eventually you can write their names for them to use as an example or coach them in some of the conventions of lines and circles, spacing, and size for different letters. Keep a collection of these writing samples to study the children's evolving awareness and skill. This will guide you in knowing what scaffolding might be useful for what they can strive for next. Ask yourself questions such as these:

1   Do the children show they understand the difference between writing and drawing?

2   Do they pretend to write by making lines or scribbles?

3   Do they make marks for separate words or use one long, cursive line?

4   Do they know how to make some of the letters of their name?

5   How do they place the letters of their name—in order or randomly?

Though many of the children don't share the same home language, they are still eager to communicate in writing with each other. We started a friendship card writing project with another center in our neighborhood and sent the card home with the children as well. Elias's dad explained to me that Elias would get home from preschool and start writing all the names down until he was able to write them down without help from him or the list. He was very good at writing the names down, and in each area of the classroom, we would find Elias's list of names. During circle time, Elias would spell out the names of his friends (out loud), and they would seek him for assistance in writing their names.   —KARINA, TEACHER

You can assess what children know about writing by comparing your analysis with resources on the developmental stages of writing, including the Lieberman citation. These appear in the second edition of our book *Reflecting Children's Lives*.

More Things to Do

The more you do to explore your own understandings of the representational and decoding process to communicate, the better you can support these processes with children. Try the following activities to gain more experience with the representational process.

Practice Other Forms of Representation

Outside of basic writing and shorthand notes and symbols, many of us haven't developed our representational skills. In fact, our lack of support for this development has left many adults feeling we aren't creative. We are intimidated when asked to work with art materials, play music, or read dramatically. It often hasn't occurred to us that art materials can be tools for thinking and processing feelings and ideas.

Invest some time exploring various materials such as watercolors, clay, and wire, and other forms of expressing ideas such as rap, haiku poems, and improvisational theater activities. Take a workshop or class on these expressive arts as part of your professional development to deepen your understanding of supporting children's efforts.

Experiment with Decoding Symbolic Representations

Use this activity to gain more insight into how children learn to decode abstract symbols. From your public library or the Internet, gather some of the following items for you and your partner or group to examine:

X-rays	pictures of sign language
examples of Braille	Morse code
Egyptian hieroglyphics	diagrams of technology or
cave drawings	satellite photography
samples of Japanese calligraphy	

Work together to decode the meaning or story of each, discussing these questions:

1 What clues helped you decipher the meaning of this story?

2 If you were to tell it as a story, what would you say about this?

3 What could you do to further explore your hunches about the meaning?

4 How does this activity give you insight into your work with children?

Explore Representing to Learn

College instructor Tom Drummond developed an earlier version of this activity to explore how we learn in collaboration with others and represent our theories in drawings. Collect a variety of objects that have some hidden, movable parts as part of their function, such as a kitchen timer, pen with a variety of ink colors, wind-up toys, combination lock, Etch-A-Sketch drawing toy, kaleidoscope, or staple gun. Work with a partner or a small group and choose one of the objects to examine. Follow this procedure in exploring your object:

1   Look at the object closely, exploring and noticing all of the mechanisms and features that make it work. At first, try to do this without talking. Do not take the item apart.

2   Share your ideas with one another about how you think the object works. Try demonstrating to one another by manipulating the object or using your body to show your ideas.

3   Take a few minutes to sketch your own theory of how the object works. You can use other materials to make it two- or three-dimensional, if that helps.

4   Share your drawings with one another and see if any of your theories changes or is supported.

5   Discuss how each of the forms of representation (discussion, demonstration, and drawing) assisted with your learning about the object.

6   Discuss the role that other people played in helping you understand. What else would have been helpful?

7   Talk about how this experience relates to children's use of representation in learning and what they need from teachers in their writing.

Sample Observation Display

As you read the story of two-year-old Cole, study the pictures carefully. Notice the details of what he has done with the playdough as well as how he uses his hands and face to communicate his understandings. When teachers capture and display moments like this for others to see, they help them look more closely and deepen their appreciation of all the ways children show us what is on their minds.

Cole Connects Symbols with Ideas

In the two-year-old room, Cole was working at the dough table for at least ten minutes before I sat down at the table beside him. He seemed very engaged, and I was curious about what was

capturing his attention for so long. I was tempted to ask him what he was doing but decided just to watch for a minute to see what I could learn. His hands were wrapped around a chunk of playdough that he was squeezing together into a ball. He then put it on the table and leaned his whole body forward, giving his hand more pressure to flatten out the ball he had just made. Next, he picked up the nearby cookie cutter and pressed that into the dough, again leaning his whole body in. I was impressed with how knowledgeable and skilled he seemed to be at this process, but what he did next really astounded me. Cole put his thumb and forefinger up beside his cheek and started singing, "Tweet-tweet, tweet-tweet." At that point, I followed his eyes down to the playdough and saw the impression he had made. "You made a bird!" I exclaimed. Again, he put his fingers together up by his cheek and sang the bird song again. My mind immediately went to what I've learned in child development classes—that concrete objects help children learn symbolic relations. Here Cole was not only recognizing the iconic shape of a bird in the dough (even looking at it upside down!), but he went on to demonstrate that he knew how birds move their beaks and sing. Cole stirred both my heart and mind.

And what did Cole do next? He gave me butterflies! He chose another cutter and pressed it carefully and firmly into the dough, again showing his intention of making an imprint. Then he lifted his arms up and down and said, "Flying, flying," looking around as if he might be trying to find a place nearby to land. I looked down at the dough, and there was an imprint of a butterfly.

As adults, we're often so focused on getting children to use words at this age, and developing a growing vocabulary is, of course, very important. But by representing what he knows in another language, using his body and sound for bird song and flapping arms to represent butterfly wings, Cole taught me to pay closer attention. He reminded me of how much more young children know and understand than we adults give them credit for, especially when they aren't yet fluent speakers.

Cole is already demonstrating a close connection to other living things, not to mention showing us he's developing symbolic thinking, a prerequisite for academic skills and the arts. Because Cole is so clearly able to recognize symbols for things that aren't concretely present, the idea of letters standing for sounds will no doubt be easy for him to grasp. We can readily see his visual discrimination at work, noticing the difference between birds and butterflies. This will serve him well in learning to read as well.

I wonder if Cole has a special affinity for creatures that fly and how we could find out more. I'll talk to the other teachers about additional props that could be brought in to explore this possibility. We could even add written words with these props to see if Cole shows an interest in them.

At two years old, Cole is a focused learner and eager to communicate what he knows. How lucky I was to see his lively mind at work.

—MARGIE, TEACHER

Chapter 10

Study Session: Observing How Children Form Relationships and Negotiate Conflict

A flower is relatively small. Everyone has many associations with a flower—the idea of flowers. You put out your hand to touch the flower—lean forward to smell it—maybe touch it with your lips almost without thinking—or give it to someone to please them. Still—in a way—nobody sees a flower—really—it is so small— we haven't time—and to see takes time, like to have a friend takes time.
—GEORGIA O'KEEFFE

Learning Goals for This Study Session

In this study session you will
- practice looking attentively, using contour drawings
- recall important relationships from your childhood
- relish the warmth and kindness that children bring to relationships
- examine what you learned about conflict in your childhood
- practice seeing relationships and conflict from children's perspectives

Reflect on the Quote

Georgia O'Keeffe reminds us of the importance of time in making connections and seeing the world. Use these questions to guide your reflections on her words:
- What does this quote mean to you?
- What recent experience does it remind you of?
- How does this quote relate to your work with children?

Do some reflective writing and talk with another person or a group about your thinking. You might want to use the teacher responses below to spark or extend your thinking.

I feel that this quote relates to seeing things only on the surface. Most people don't notice the beauty in the world. We are in such a hurry to get from place to place that we forget the simple pleasures of hearing birds singing or seeing the bright blue sky on a clear day. I have been practicing my observation skills by stepping out of the fray and taking time to really look closely at one particular child or one area of the room. It makes me realize how much I miss when I'm only looking at the surface.—BECKY, PRESCHOOL TEACHER

I am struck by the last line about the time it takes to have a friend. It relates so much to what we have been studying in this class. To be with children and ourselves in meaningful ways takes time. I want to slow down and have enough time to form relationships with what I see, with the children and grown-ups around me, and with myself.—LaVonda, ECE student

Art of Awareness Activity

Draw the Contours

In *Learning by Heart*, Corita Kent and Jan Steward recommend the use of contour drawings to enhance our ability to see things the way artists do. When we look at the world and label its phenomena, we often make immediate appraisals. We like something or dislike it. We accept it or reject it according to our ideas about its usefulness to us. We judge it based on some criteria from our past experiences. But to really see takes time and letting go of all of our preconceived notions. One of the ways artists cultivate their ability to see is by using contour drawings. Contour drawings are made with keen attention to the object to be drawn, not looking at your paper or the drawing you are making. This practice develops your ability to see and ultimately enhances your ability to draw.

Creating and analyzing are two different processes and can't be done at the same time. This is true about contour drawing and also about observing children. It is impossible to really observe and see what is there when you are attempting to analyze what is happening at the same time. To practice letting go of analysis when you observe, try to let go of your expectations of the outcome for your drawing. Concentrate on learning to see the many details of the object you are trying to draw. Do this drawing very slowly. Begin by trying to see your hand as you draw its contours.

1   Find a place where you can be uninterrupted for at least fifteen minutes.

2   Sit at a table that is a comfortable height for drawing. Place a blank piece of paper on the table in front of you. You may want to tape the paper down so it doesn't move while you draw.

3   Put the point of your pencil on the paper in front of you, and turn your body away from the paper so you cannot see the paper or the hand you are drawing with.

4   Look at your other hand. Pick some part of the hand to start with, and let your eye follow the outline and details of your hand. Your eye must move very slowly. At the same time, move the pencil point along the paper, reproducing every tiny detail of the line of your hand as your eye follows it. Be careful not to let either your eye or the pencil get ahead.

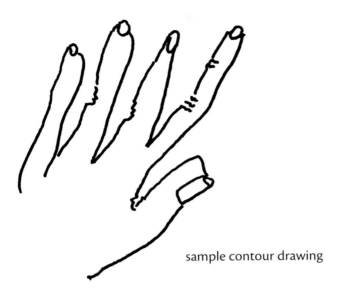

sample contour drawing

5   Rather than seeing your hand, look at the shapes and lines your hand is made up of. Draw the details of what you see without looking at the paper or lifting your pencil point until you are done.

6   Reflect on your experience. How did it feel to draw without looking? Were you able to look closely at the details of your hand and let your pencil follow?

Learn to See Childhood as a Time of Building Relationships

The significant people and the time we spent with them are probably our most meaningful childhood experiences. Everything we know about children says that the best way for them to grow up is within a loving, nurturing family and community. In the jargon of professional early childhood programs, we describe these experiences in the following ways:

- developing social skills
- building self-esteem
- learning strategies to ease separation anxiety
- learning techniques for guidance and discipline
- managing conflict

Instead of adopting the clinical mind-set revealed in these terms, we should focus our attention on the friendships and conflicts that are unfolding with the children. As professionals, we have to be vigilant that we don't reduce these important experiences and connections to the jargon of professional discourse, assessment checklists, and management techniques.

A better strategy is to call on the memories of our own meaningful relationships and seek to create similar conditions that foster connections and warm feelings in our daily work with children. The next activity is designed to help you remember a heartfelt relationship you had as a child.

Practice Remembering an Important Relationship

Choose a particular person from your childhood who had a positive and significant influence on your life. This can be a grown-up or another child. Think about and describe that person in as much detail as you can remember, using these questions to guide your memory. You can either write this on your own or talk with a partner or small group.

1   Describe this person's physical appearance: hands, hair, eyes, smell, clothing, tone of voice, and body language.

2   What did you do together?

3   What did this person do well, and how did this person share himself with you?

4   How did this person express affection or love for you?

5   How did you feel about yourself when you were with this person? Why?

6   What did you learn both directly and indirectly from this person that stays with you to this day?

7   Think about your own relationships with children in your group. In what ways are you sharing yourself with them as this person did with you?

Practice Remembering a Childhood Conflict

Our challenge in observing children's conflicts is to identify our own tension and discomfort, which often come from past experiences or preconceptions about conflict situations. To see these moments clearly, we need to become aware of the personal baggage that could be clouding our view. The next activity will help you reflect on these issues. Think back to your childhood and remember some incidents that involved you in a conflict or in which you observed a conflict in your family. If you experienced abuse or extreme pain or hurt in your childhood, you can choose to skip this activity. Such experiences should be healed through counseling or other personal work so they don't interfere with your ability to clearly see children's conflicts for what they are.

1   What happened in the conflict you remember? What did people do or say?

2   How did people respond to your expression of feelings?

3   What did you learn about conflict from your experiences and what people said to you, either directly or indirectly?

4   How do you think about conflict now?

5   How do you think your childhood experiences and messages influence your responses to conflict now?

Use the insights from your own memories of a special relationship and conflict to examine the following observations of children involved in developing relationships with each other and with adults.

I Want My Dolly Back!

Jill, the teacher in the toddler room, is sitting on the carpet with Angelic and Krystal as they play together with a soft stuffed elephant. Karl wanders over and sits facing Angelic. He sees the stuffed elephant and reaches for it. Angelic lets out a piercing scream— "No!"—as she clutches the elephant tighter.

Teacher Jill urges Karl to ask Angelic if he can play too. He looks at her and asks, "Me play?"

Angelic screeches angrily in Karl's face. "No!"

Karl punches her in the arm and grabs the elephant. Both children hold on for dear life, and a tug-of-war ensues.

Angelic begins kicking Karl and hitting him with her free hand, screaming, "I want my dolly back. I want my dolly back." He responds by hitting her back several times.

Krystal, an onlooker at this point, punches Karl from the other side. He begins to flail his free arm in her direction, still holding on to the elephant. Krystal responds by kicking him.

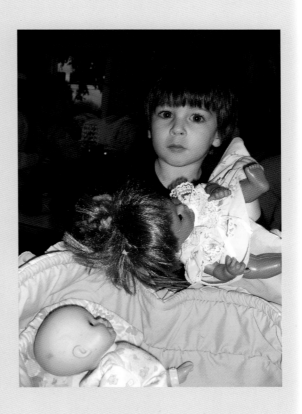

Having watched this unfold in a matter of seconds, Teacher Jill lifts Krystal to her side, away from the fray, and then disengages Karl's hand from the elephant. Karl crawls away from the scene. As he turns to go, Jill begins to speak to him. He looks straight into her face and makes a fierce growling shout, drowning out what she is trying to tell him.

Jill turns her attention back to Krystal and Angelic, who are both involved in nonstop crying. They are crying in unison, following each other's long, woeful moans. Jill suggests, "Would you like to go to the mirror and look at your sad faces? You are both so sad." They get up and go to the mirror, still lamenting, but now watching their own facial expressions as they cry. "Look at how sad your faces are. You even have tears," Jill points out. Karl joins them at the mirror, looking quizzically at the girls' faces along with them.

—DEB, TEACHER (OBSERVER)

Work alone, with a partner, or in a small group to discuss the details of this story to find the meaning. Put yourself in each of these children's shoes, using the following questions as a guide.

1   What do each of the children seem to understand about the situation?

2   What do each of them feel strongly about?

3   What strategies do they use to get what they want?

4   What did you learn about each of the children from the details?

5   What is your reaction to how the teacher handled this situation?

6   How do you think the children felt about the teacher's response?

In the midst of a conflict, especially when children are screaming, crying, hitting, and kicking, many teachers find their hearts starting to pound. Our heads fill with adult sentiments of justice and fairness, our serious responsibility to keep children safe, and our duty to teach them how they should behave and get along. Buried beneath all these thoughts are the responses we learned from our own childhoods, messages we received about expressing strong feelings and taking part in conflicts. Needless to say, it is extremely difficult to get past our own filters and biases to the present children's perspectives and understandings.

Throughout this book, you have read the message that childhood is a time of wonder. It is also a time of raw, uncensored emotions, a time of uncertainty, insecurity, and many fears. The ability to observe conscientiously, looking for children's points of view and understandings, is critical in these situations. During intense incidents such as the one described by Teacher Jill, children are constructing ideas about who they are. In essence, they are forming their identities. Teachers need to approach conflicts as clearly and openly as possible to help children through these scary times.

Take some time to study how Jill is approaching this tumultuous incident. Jill sees her role in this conflict as a storyteller, attempting to make the children's ideas and feelings visible. She doesn't try to fix their behavior or emotions. She tries to keep the children physically safe as best she can. And rather than pursuing who was right or wrong, she follows the most prominent theme: the crying girls. Thoughtfully, she tells and shows them the story of their own feelings and, in the process, helps them see each other's more clearly. This gets Karl's attention without her having to single him out as the perpetrator of hurtful behavior. For toddlers, the most meaningful place to begin conflict negotiation is with their feelings.

You can negotiate these difficult times, along with the joyful moments, by continually being mindful of your own mental filters and biases and focusing on the children's perspectives and understandings. Children have the right to wrestle through the difficult moments of childhood with adult respect and support for the full expression of their strong feelings.

"I See You!"

Snuggled together in the big stroller, my group of toddlers and I head to the park near our child care center. There is plenty of space to explore and run, and the children approach the park with eager anticipation. Located in the middle of the park is an interesting concrete structure that was installed to be a water park in the summertime. Although it wasn't designed for toddlers, this structure is a magical world to them.

The children are enchanted with the space as they move through it, immersed and surrounded by the white walls and whimsical openings. The structure has different levels, so the children are challenged to move and climb as they look up, down, and through the holes. They are rapt with attention to every detail—the shadows, shapes, textures, and different views from each opening—which offers endless opportunities for their exploration and delight.

They invented a game over time that now they play every day. The children play peekaboo, again and again, taking turns looking through the holes. Their elated laughter rings out when they peek around a corner and see a friend. Each time they encounter one another, the children radiate feelings of pure joy from the simple realization that they see each other.

—DEB, TEACHER

Reflect on this story alone or with a partner or a group. Use these questions to guide your thinking.

1   What understandings do you think the children are exploring and expressing?

2   What are the children's points of view in this story?

3   How do they see their connections and relationships with others?

In his article "The Infant as Reflection of Soul," William M. Schafer (2004) suggests that babies are born with three spiritual dimensions that we no longer experience as adults and that many people try to reclaim through spiritual practices such as prayer and meditation. He describes these as

- **Presence:** approaching life with pure awareness, free from internal judgment, comparison, fear, or desire

- **Joy:** a strong sense of being drawn toward something or someone in wonder, curiosity, and interest

- **Awareness of others' awareness:** the realization that we are not alone and that others exist who are present to our experiences

As you read Deb's story of the toddler peekaboo game, do you recognize some of what Schafer describes? Try looking for this in the children you work with. If you continually focus your observation on the details of children's joy in connecting with others, you, too, might find the same pleasure in the simple yet powerful message "I see you."

Consider Children's Relationships with You

In your work with young children, you may be the first adult outside of their families to have a significant relationship with them. If you work in a child care program, it's likely that children will spend more of their time with you than with their families. By nature, children are eager to connect with you, to gain your attention, support, and approval. They are born with the skills of social scientists seeking to establish relationships for warmth and survival. They are keen observers, learning your ways in the world so they know how to feel accepted, safe, and cared for. Observing children closely for skills and competence as they establish a relationship with you increases your abilities to support and connect with them. As you read the following observation examples, notice the children's perspectives and their ability to connect with their teachers. In addition, look for how their teachers see and support the children's remarkable capacity for empathy, responsibility, and connections.

"All Clean"

Today Lukas spent quite a bit of time in the diaper-changing area with the baby dolls. I originally approached him to see if he needed a diaper change, but when I heard him engaging in pretend play, I stepped back and observed the following.

Lukas was talking to the baby doll, saying things such as "No poop?" and "All clean?" Initially, he was changing the baby on the small changing table outside of the bathroom. But after a few minutes of play, he inched toward the bathroom, where the real changing table is located. "Come out?" Lukas asked me as he tugged on one of the diapers. "New one on?" he insisted. I pointed to the small basket of diapers for the dolls next to the small changing table. Immediately Lukas took the smaller diaper and climbed up to the big changing table and began to change his

doll. He had a bit of difficulty but enjoyed my help as he stayed with the task until he was successful and exclaimed proudly, "All clean!" I really loved the time I spent with Lukas this morning. Something as simple as a diaper change turned into a learning experience for both of us! His competence and the way he showed how he connects with me truly amazed me.—LINDSAY, TEACHER

In this story of Lukas and his teacher, Lindsay, we see the importance of daily routines, such as diaper changing, for building relationships. Children are eager to have close relationships with their teachers and to feel cared for in the environment. They are keen observers of our actions, body language, tone of voice, and facial expressions. Two-year-old Lukas shows us the bond he has built with Lindsay and the closeness and comfort he feels as he imitates her interactions with him with his doll. This diaper-changing drama becomes their avenue for sharing responsibility, playfulness, and a growing friendship.

"I Have to Tell You Something"

Today Bella tentatively approached Teacher Simone in the yard. She walked slowly, head bowed, hands behind her back. She looked sad, as if she had something on her mind. As she came closer, Simone kneeled on the ground and opened her arms, communicating a willingness to help.

When Simone embraced her, Bella explained, "I have to tell you something."

"I would love to hear what's on your mind," Simone offered.

Bella pulled out a pencil sharpener from behind her back and handed it to Simone, whispering, "I broke it."

They examined the pencil sharpener together. It seemed that although the sharpener had broken off of the container, the blades were still intact and could be safely used on their own. Bella and Simone discussed how they might still be able to use the sharpener if they held it over a wastebasket to catch the pencil shavings. They tested their hypothesis and discovered the sharpener did in fact still function properly. Bella smiled with relief when she successfully sharpened a pencil. She even giggled when she witnessed the shavings fall into the garbage can.

They returned the sharpener to a shelf in the writing center, and Bella turned to hug Simone and began to cry. Trembling, she pushed her body into Simone's, gripping her tightly, seeking comfort and reassurance. Bella's heart was pounding inside her chest. Tears of relief were streaming down her face.

—SIMONE, EARLY CHILDHOOD TEACHER

Read Simone's reflections on this encounter with Bella.

I was surprised to see how emotional Bella was, even though she found out that the sharpener still worked. That's when I realized how anxious and scared she must have felt about telling me of her mishap. Did she think she was in trouble? Did she expect me to be angry with her? I can see from her actions in this moment that she has fostered a sense of belonging here in our program. She considers herself part of our learning community. She understands the boundaries of acceptable behavior at our school and assumes responsibility for her actions. I also see how much we have established a relationship, because she was so willing to share this painful moment with me. Through this experience, I was reminded of how difficult it can be to be honest and tell the truth—especially when implicating oneself! Experiencing such deep emotions will allow Bella to grow empathetic toward others.

Take Another Look

Most teachers are very invested in helping children learn to get along, feel accepted, and solve conflicts. Because this is an area of human development where emotions run deep for both adults and children, it is one that benefits from ongoing study and reflection. It is useful to observe the ways children are already competent in developing relationships, as the following observation, "Sharing Is Caring," reflects.

Sharing Is Caring

When Katja started working in the program, the first words she heard Caroline saying were "Sharing is caring." Since then, Caroline has clearly made it visible that she practices what she preaches. Every morning, when she is busy at the playdough table making treats like muffins, cookies, or pies, she offers them to her friends who are playing with her, asking, "Would you like some?" Other days, when Caroline wants to play with the same toy that another child is playing with, she requests in a simple, gentle voice, "You have two, can I have one?" Even though Caroline appears nervous, she is working to make connections with others by asking, "Do you want to be my friend?" Caroline is also growing a relationship with her teacher, Katja. Every morning when they see each other, Caroline asks Katja about her mismatched socks. She races over to Katja, excitedly calling out, "Miss Katjaaa!" Then she grabs her leg and gives her a hug. They have developed a routine in which they first talk about mismatched socks, then give each other a morning hug, and finally Caroline helps Katja set up activities on the playground.

Here are Katja's reflections on Caroline's capacity to build relationships.

Caroline's kindness when playing and communicating with others is wonderful to see! Seeing her awareness of others in the classroom and watching her use kind words with her peers are inspiring to me. I can see that through her sharing and openness to communicate, she really wants and understands how to make connections with peers and teachers. It has been a delight getting to know her, and I can't wait to watch her continue to grow.—KATJA, TEACHER

Observe Children Finding Playmates

Identify two different children—a child who enters play with others easily and another who struggles with this. Then observe them over the course of a week or so. Watch as they approach or are approached in play situations, indoors and out. How do they respond? What words, body language, and strategies do they use? Write down the details and compare the differences between the two children.

Observe the Language of Friendship

Observe a small group of children who typically play together. Listen and record their conversations and interactions related to their friendships. Remember to notice the language of gestures and negotiations. Do you hear any repeated phrases that indicate their efforts to understand what it means to be a friend? Remember to seek their point of view rather than your own agenda for how they should be behaving.

Observe for Conflicts and Problem Solving

Make note of the conflicts that occur among the children in your group over the course of a week. Try to analyze each by looking for the details and the children's point of view, using the following questions to guide your thinking.

1   Are there any patterns in the sources of these conflicts?
2   What seem to be the children's understandings?
3   What strategies do they use to get what they want?
4   Notice and reflect on your own reactions to these conflicts and interactions. Is there anything from your own childhood that influences how you see these situations?

More Things to Do

As you work to see children's relationships more closely, also devote time to explore your own experience with developing relationships. This will give you more insight into this process with children.

Think of a Friendship You've Developed as an Adult

Identify someone outside of your family with whom you've developed a friendship as an adult.

Try to remember how this happened. What kinds of things did you do together that helped you become friends? How did you spend time together? What did you offer each other? How have you handled differences between you? What helped you develop trust and affection?

Remember Difficult Moments in Relationships

All of us have had times with other people when things didn't go well. As you recall particular experiences, consider how you felt and what you tried to do to resolve the situation. See if you can uncover any new insights into children's behaviors. Try using this list to organize your memories.

- Remember a time when your feelings were hurt by someone you trusted.

- Remember a time that you broke something that belonged to someone else.

- Remember a time when you were rebuffed or excluded from a relationship or activity.

- Remember a time when you were tricked or lied to.

- Remember a time when you felt misunderstood.

Practice More Contour Drawings

To continue expanding your ability to see details, do at least ten more contour drawings as described in the Art of Awareness Activity section of this chapter.

Sample Observation Display

In the following observation story, a group of teachers who have been researching their work together created a documentation display to show their learning and discoveries. Imagine a parent or visitor reading the details of the children's collaboration. What might they learn about children? How would their view of children be affected?

Teacher Research—Learning Together

What We Planned

Our toddler teacher group worked together to plan an experience for a group of toddlers to explore the natural world right outside their classroom door. We have been studying toddlers together for a while. We eagerly anticipated using our observation and documentation to see what would unfold with the children immersed in the wonders of nature. We spread a blanket on the ground and brought out some trays and baskets. We used the natural materials we collected on the playground to create a beautiful invitation to share with the children. Our plan was to study the children's response and engagement with these interesting items from the natural world.

What We Observed

Toddlers often have a reputation for a lack of self-control and short attention span, so we were surprised when the children didn't dive right in to play with the materials. They were definitely curious about the group of teachers waiting for them as well as the treasures we offered. A couple of the children approached the invitation gradually with looks of curiosity and a bit of wariness in their eyes. The other children held back, watching their peers. The two adventurous children eagerly studied, touched, rubbed, and manipulated the objects. Their bodies and facial expressions relaxed in response to the friendly adults and their strong

desire to engage with these new objects This seemed to be a cue to the other children that it was safe to join in. The children continued observing each other closely and began to learn from each other's actions and investigations. The toddlers worked with a quiet focus and determination and rapt attention to the activities unfolding around them. When one child took up the magnifying glass, others quickly followed and learned to use it as well. When another child began to smell the berries, several other children put the berries and leaves up to their noses to smell them. The shared exploration continued as children's close study to learn from one another prompted a variety of explorations and new discoveries. This included making sounds by shaking the leaves, tapping the rocks together, and dropping the pods on the trays and into the wooden bowls. Each of their investigations inspired further actions. Dropping objects into bowls evolved into careful sorting and arranging of the berries and plums into the bowls and baskets. A few of the children seemed to be noticing and classifying by size as they placed the berries in the containers. As toddlers often do, their attention turned to exuberant ways to make the natural objects move. This developed into a group effort as the children invented a game together to roll and bounce the green berries on the large black trays. They laughed uproariously, shaking the tray until all of the berries flew off. Then they enthusiastically filled the tray and started the game again. After more than an hour, we reluctantly interrupted the children's exploration for lunch.

What We Learned

Our focus of studying how children engage with the natural world proved fruitful. The children's explorations helped us learn right along with them about the beauty of nature's patterns, textures, sounds, and smells. They showed us the roots of scientific inquiry as they reminded us how to use our senses to examine and make discoveries, to try out ideas, to notice cause and effect, and to realize the impact our actions have on the world around us. They gave us the gift of seeing the joy, mystery, and excitement in the simple beauty of nature.

But what stood out to us most was their attention to one another and the reminder that at the heart of all of life's experiences is our connections with others. We could see the children had strong bonds that allowed them to feel safe and comfortable enough in this unfamiliar situation to join in. We saw how much they used each other's ideas to build on their own thinking and learning. And we marveled at their generosity to welcome us in the comfort, joy, and delight they took in learning together.

—LINDA, KASONDRA, PATRICIA, DIANA, VALERIE, AND DEB,
TODDLER COHORT TEACHERS

Chapter 11

Study Session: Observing Children with Their Families

You don't really understand human nature unless you know why a child on a merry-go-round will wave at his parents every time around—and why his parents will always wave back.

—WILLIAM TAMMEUS

Learning Goals for This Study Session

In this study session, you will

- practice using mirrors to take different perspectives
- recall the influences of your family and family life on your attitudes and values
- examine the similarities and differences of values and attitudes between you and the families you work with
- practice observing the details of children's connections with their families
- practice seeing a parent's point of view

Reflect on the Quote

Reflect on the quote above from William Tammeus. Try to picture the scene he is describing to capture the deep bonds between children and parents at this stage of life. Consider these questions as you write your reflections on what Tammeus says:

1   What do you understand about the significance of this waving at each other again and again as the merry-go-round turns?

2   In what other ways have you identified the deep bonds that young children and their families have with each other?

3   Have you seen examples of daily rituals that young children and their families develop to express their bonds and keep them connected during times when they aren't together?

4   What rituals could you develop to help children stay connected to their families as they separate and come together each day in your program?

Consider this teacher's response to the quote to provoke your thinking further.

I believe that all children and parents have deep bonds with each other, even though circumstances may sometimes make it difficult for these to be expressed in a loving way. To me, one important reason for any ritual, especially during times of separation, is to create a strong memory of shared love and bonds that can be turned to in times of uncertainty. This can be reassuring to both children and parents, and it can be specifically helpful to us as teachers when those early morning separations are tearful. We have a ritual where the child and parent hold their fingers in front of their faces and squint one eye, pretending to take a photo of each other as a way of saying "I'll keep you with me when we are apart." As children and families learn this ritual, they come to use it each day and love it.—WILLIAM, PRESCHOOL TEACHER

Art of Awareness Activity

Explore Mirrors

Whether we recognize it or not, most of us move about in the world with perspectives strongly shaped by how we grew up. We might not be aware of how these influences affect our view of other people, whose lives are quite different from ours. The following activity using mirrors offers the opportunity to explore visual perceptions in interesting ways. For young children, studying images in mirrors actually develops their brains so that they more easily see things from different points of view. When adults use mirrors, we, too, stretch our brains' capacity to see different perspectives.

Gather a collection of mirrors of different sizes and shapes. Mylar mirror foil is good to include as well. Try arranging the mirrors to explore how they shift the way you see things. You can explore your mirrors in the following ways.

1   Hold two of the mirrors together at a right angle with the edges touching so you can open and close them like a book. Hold the mirrors close enough to see an image of your face across both mirrors. Slowly open and close the mirrors, watching for a progressive number of images of yourself. What sensation does this leave you with?

2   Place a mirror perpendicular to a piece of paper on a table in front of you. Try writing your name on the paper, looking only in the mirror as you write. What happens with your perception?

3   On another piece of paper, draw a wavelike line, then looking only in the mirror, try to trace the line on the paper with your finger. Why do you think this is challenging?

4   Now try using pattern blocks to create a design while looking in the mirror. Pay attention to the duplicate image you see in your mirror, and use that to guide the development of your design. How does this task require you to use your brain differently?

Take some time to write about or discuss your experience with a partner or small group. What did you notice was easy or difficult for you? How do you think this relates to learning to see things from different perspectives?

Learn to See Childhood as a Time for Strong Family Connections

Each of the mirror activities asks you to try seeing things in ways that aren't typical. This is exactly what you need to learn when observing and working with children and their families. Childhood is a time of experiencing yourself as part of a family. Children get their first identity and sense of belonging in their families. They may acquire an endearing nickname or hear who they look like, what their grandma used to do, and a series of stories about what life was like for their parents growing up. If they are adopted, children learn a particular story of how they became part of the family they will grow up in. A sense of history and affiliation evolves through these interactions and stories. Unless we understand these family situations, we can't really know the full measure of a child or provide continuity for them when they are with us.

Each child joins a family that has its own values, customs, community, and internal dynamics. Whatever the family makeup or circumstances, almost all parents start off with hopes and dreams for their child. Perhaps the family is not fully conscious or intentional about what they want to pass on to their child, but family dynamics and patterns will strongly influence the child's functioning and self-concept.

When a family enrolls their child in one of our programs, we are often concerned with how they will separate from the family and bond with the new caregivers. Separation anxiety is the focus of a great number of staff discussions and workshops. As we begin to recognize that children today are spending more of their waking hours in our programs than with their families, we should be working to help children stay connected to their families rather than focusing on their separation.

Whānau Activity

In Aotearoa, New Zealand, we learn the Maori concept of not only keeping children connected to their immediate family but to *whānau*, the wider family community spanning several generations. Educator Thelma Chapman explains, "Though each child is unique, he/she is surrounded by *whānau* (family), both visible and invisible, living and dead, the product of his/her genealogical heritage. The fabric of the *whānau* is multilayered and encompasses not just the parents and siblings but is intergenerational including grandparents, aunties, uncles, cousins, and wider. Everyone shares in the responsibility and well-being of the child. Embedded in the notion of *whānau* are the concepts of identity and belonging. In the early childhood field, we talk about having a child-centered approach, but in a Maori context, it is *whānau*-centered of which the child is the focus. This is common to many indigenous communities, where the welfare of the *whānau* was paramount for survival. It would be logical, therefore, that what was good for the *whānau* would also benefit the child."

On your own, with a partner or in a small group, reflect on the Maori concept of *whānau,* using these questions to guide you:

1   How similar to or different from your experience is this concept of one's identity being derived from multigenerational, extended family?

2   What changes might you make in your work with children and families if you were to shape your practice with inspiration from the Maori concept of *whānau*?

Whatever the level of diversity in your program, do not assume that staff and parents share common perspectives and values with regard to child-rearing practices. Differences may exist as a result of personal preference, culture, economic conditions, life experiences, and age or generation factors. These different perspectives may contribute to misunderstandings, if not judgments, of one another. To build strong partnerships with children's families, you can apply the same awareness and observation skills you use with children to discover indicators of family values, traditions, and communication styles. Approaching families with a mind-set of curiosity, suspended judgment, and eagerness to learn will help you build trust. It will also support the needed continuity and connections between children and their families.

Just as your interpretation of children's behaviors can be clouded by your own childhood experiences, so your view of their relationships with their families can be similarly obscured. Remembering adult influences that supported your identity development will help you value the ways that families support their children's identities. Use the following activity to reflect on your own childhood influences.

Identifying Affirming Connections in Your Childhood

Think about the people in your family or close circle of friends who had strong, affirming influences on you as you were growing up. Whether you grew up with your biological family or in a foster or surrogate family, or didn't have a warm or close family experience, consider one particular person from your childhood who had a very positive influence on you. Use these questions to help you describe this person, either in writing or to a partner or in a small group.

- Describe the person's hands, voice, smell, and clothing.

- What did this person share with or teach you?

- How did this person impress you with a lasting memory?

- How did this person let you know you were loved and cared for?

- What did this person teach you that still influences you today?

Next, consider the traditions of your family or close friends. What are some of the most touching and important rituals, values, and activities that came from your past experiences with these people that you have developed and kept alive through the years?

Reflect on these two memory activities and about the values and beliefs you bring to your work with young children. Consider these questions.

1   Are these the same as or different from what you know about the families of the children you work with?

2   What are the values and experiences you share with the families?

3   What differences do you see in your values and experiences? How can you account for these differences?

Using your new awareness about your own family experiences, see what else you can discover from the following observation stories about children's relationships with their families.

A Shelter for the Animal Family

Today I found Jorja in the block area with some props she had gathered to create a story about animal families. She began by arranging the animals on beds of playdough, ensuring that each had a place, and then carefully measuring to ensure that each animal had an adequate shelter, which she called a tent. She spent quite a bit of time arranging and rearranging these animal beds,

describing how they needed to be in just the right place and that she would keep them safe. Standing on the sidelines, watching and taking notes, at one point Jorja's teacher offered her a camera. Jorja approached her role as the family photographer with the same care she had as the family caregiver, bending down to get different approaches and angles to the animals in their tents. She made sure that each got featured in a picture. —CHERYL, TEACHER

Taking Care of Celina

This week, Sophia's sister, Celina, started at our center. This transition was difficult for her as she is still very young and had never been in school before. As Celina's big sister, Sophia took it upon herself to protect and care for her, to show her sister all her favorite places to play, and guide her through transitions. Despite Sophia's efforts to keep her engaged, Celina continued to have a difficult time, and Sophia dedicated her days to tending to Celina's needs—cuddling and hugging her, offering her toys to play with, opening her lunch box for her, and translating English into Mandarin. Sophia even wiped Celina's eyes and nose for her with a tissue when she cried! I have never seen a child wipe another's nose in such a gentle and endearing manner.

I want to make sure we let Sophia know that, just as she cares for Celina, the children and teachers at our center care about her, and we will always be right there to help her when she needs us.—SIMONE, EARLY CHILDHOOD TEACHER

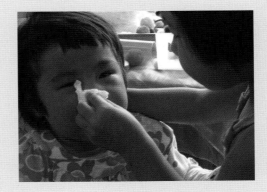

Work on your own, with a partner, or in a small group to discuss these two observation stories. Consider these questions for your reflections:

1   What ideas about family do the children in each of these stories reveal in their actions?

2   If you were Cheryl or Simone, what thoughts or questions might each of these observations prompt you to discuss with the children's families?

3   How might Jorja and Sophia be acknowledged for their understandings about caregiving. How could this be useful for the other children in your program?

These stories remind us of the important role we have in helping children stay connected to their families. Children rely on grown-ups, particularly their family members, for all of their needs for belonging, security, and comfort. This is why separation from their families is such a big issue in children's lives. When you observe them closely, you can see the many ways they create opportunities to gain comfort and security. When you are aware and accept children's issues and understandings, you will find more ways to reassure them while they are away from their families.

The next two stories about teacher and parent interactions provide an opportunity for you to extend your observation practice to interactions between other adults. With a focus on the tensions that can arise from different values, these stories remind you to consider who children are in the context of the cultural perspectives of their family. As you read, pay attention to your own personal values and what might be influencing your perspective on the story.

Stay Out of the Sand

Melissa, a child care provider, believes kids learn by exploring freely, even if they do get a bit dirty in the process. She encourages the kids to play to their hearts' content when they are outside, using anything available that interests them. One of the parents has been complaining, however: "I don't want my daughter playing in your sandbox. I spent an hour and a half fixing her hair, and two minutes after she's outside, her hair is filled with sand. I can't get that stuff out, and we spend our whole evening trying to clean it up. So, please, keep her away from that sandbox and any other place on the playground where she's going to get dirty."

Potty Time

A mother and a caregiver are engaged in an intense discussion.

"I just can't do what you want," says the caregiver. "I don't have time with all of these other children to care for. Besides, I don't believe in toilet training a one-year-old."

"But she's already potty trained!" the mother says emphatically. "All you have to do is put her on the potty."

"I really don't think she's trained." The caregiver's voice is still calm, but a red flush is beginning to creep up her neck and toward her face.

"You just don't understand," says the mother, picking up her daughter and diaper bag and sweeping out the door.

"No, you're the one who doesn't understand," mutters the caregiver, busying herself with a pile of toys on the floor.

In chapter 2, "Learning to See," you reflected on the meaning of these words from Lisa Delpit, which are worth reviewing again: "We do not really see through our eyes or hear through our ears, but through our beliefs. To put our beliefs on hold is to cease to exist as ourselves for a moment."

Whether you support or disagree with the parents' or the caregivers' perspectives in these stories, try applying the ideas from Delpit when exploring the meaning of what is unfolding in these stories. Work on your own, with a partner, or with a small group, using the following questions to guide your thinking:

1 What specific details in this story give you information about each person's perspective?

2 What do the details indicate that each person values and cares about?

3 How might you summarize the contrast in their differing perspectives?

In each of the earlier study sessions of this book, you have been asked to develop an awareness of your own mental filters and point of view and to try to take the perspectives of the children you are observing. Grounded in that development, you can use the same principles to try to see the point of view of other adults. You can build trust and respect between you and a child's family by putting yourself in the family's shoes and seeing situations from the perspective of their interests and needs.

A number of resources are available to help you better understand how to work cross-culturally. A good starting place is the work of college teacher and author Janet Gonzalez-Mena, who writes about the cultural assumptions and misunderstandings that pervade early childhood programs. Most of our professional standards and knowledge about good early childhood practice have been developed from a European American perspective. Rules we make about what children need and how they should be cared for and interacted with stem from a particular perspective and set of values. Our programs need to embrace an increasing diversity of cultures, classes, languages, family structures, and disabilities, among others. We must take care not to assume that there is one right way of doing things and that parents should conform to the teacher's point of view. As you work to sensitize yourself to cross-cultural issues, keep the following questions in mind for assessing your observations:

1   What are my assumptions about the best way to handle this situation?

2   What values are influencing my point of view?

3   What evidence do I see that another set of values or assumptions are at work with this child and family?

4   How can I find out more about the family's point of view in a respectful, sensitive way?

Take Another Look

There are a number of ways you can heighten your awareness of children in the context of their families. These activities will help you explore possible strategies to use throughout your teaching day.

Be Alert to How Children Think about Their Families

Every day in your program, children incorporate feelings and themes from their family life into their play and representations. Over a week's time, gather a collection of observations and representations that reveal how children are thinking about family life. They may do this through dress-up and direct role plays, pretending to be human or animal family members. Or they may create family scenes with props as they build or play around the room. Watch and listen for what they are creating in the art area and when they have conversations or make up rhymes and songs. Looking over your week's collection, see if you can recognize any patterns or themes in your observation notes. Discuss these with coworkers to expand your understanding with other points of view.

Since early last week, Sawyer has been arriving each day with a backpack full of toy soldiers. He spends nearly all his playtime carefully placing each figure next to another. He plays alone, mostly without talking, and doesn't respond when other children ask if they can join him. Knowing that his dad has been deployed to Iraq has prompted us to create a little protective space around Sawyer, giving him the respect he needs to communicate what's going on with his family in this way.

Watch for Family Interests, Customs, and Rituals

Observe a child and family member together every day for a week or so, at either drop-off or pickup time. Notice their body language and communication style. Do they have any routines or rituals that they do day after day? Do they talk about their interests or activities? How do they greet and say good-bye to each other? How do they express emotions to each other? Do they communicate primarily through body language or with words? What details can you describe that inform you about their point of view about these interactions?

If at all possible, try visiting the family at home for an even closer look at family, interests, customs, and patterns. When this is approached as a way to strengthen partnerships rather than a requirement to gather information, families are often receptive and appreciative.

Read the following observation to see how a teacher can spot family interests in the way that children play.

Oliver's Golf Game

A few moments after entering the room, Oliver ventured over to the invitation of clear containers with a variety of round objects in them that we had set up on the floor. He collected two golf balls. I was curious about why he selected those two balls from all the other materials offered. It became obvious when he looked at me and at the golf balls and said, "Daddy!" He then chose a cylinder to drop the golf balls into. He began creating sounds and movement as he explored the cylinder and how it could be manipulated with the golf balls. Moments later, he sought out an area of the room that provided the space required to put his brilliant plan in action. He transformed the cylinder into a golf club and gently made contact with the golf ball. With great intention, he properly swung the golf club and gently launched the ball across the floor.   —SAMANTHA, TEACHER

Here's Samantha's reflection about Oliver's golfing adventure.

I was amazed by Oliver's innovative idea to transform the cylinder into a golf club. To me, this demonstrated how special Oliver's relationship is with his father. With all of the new materials and creative energy of the room, he felt it was important to let me know that he saw the connection between the golf balls and his dad. His imagination continues to inspire me to provide open-ended materials that will capture his mind. In terms of child development, I could clearly see the trajectory schema I've learned about from Piaget in how Oliver chose to use the ball. Above all, I feel his actions explained how important his relationship is with his family. I would like to provide more items that have connections to the children's families so we have the opportunity to learn more about them.

Create Family Books

Most of the paperwork we ask families to complete when they enroll their child in our program is impersonal and of limited use in helping us understand their family life. A more meaningful complement to enrollment papers are pages for the child and family to complete and add to a classroom family book. Try creating a simple form for sharing some initial information, such as pictures and stories of something special about each person in the family, something they like about where they live, and someone the family admires and talks about. Suggest that the form be filled out together as a family, using words, drawings, or photos. Offer to send home a camera as needed. The next two pages have samples of forms that can be used for this purpose.

Child's Name _____ **Birthday** _____

How I got my name

Something I love to do

What I look like

Something
I love to learn

What makes me happy   What makes me sad or mad

Family Name _____

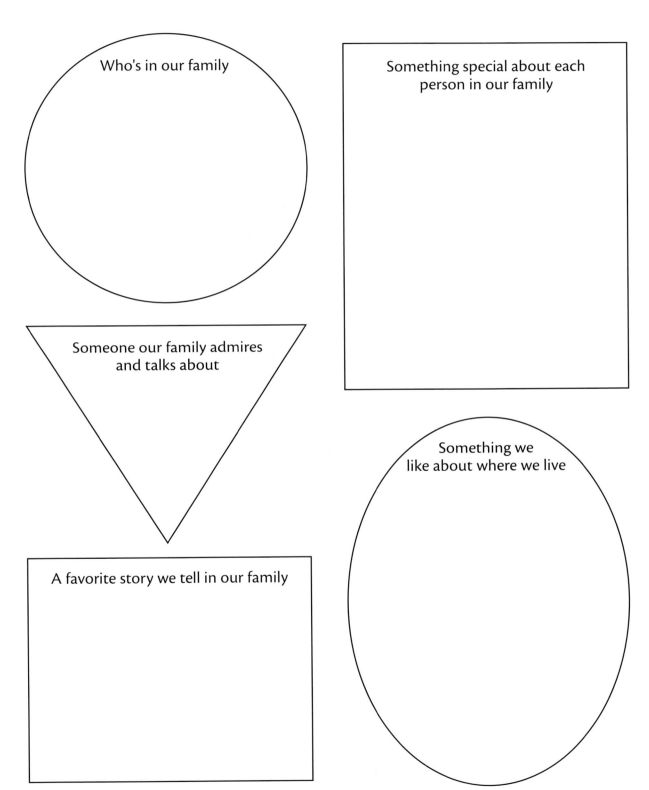

Who's in our family

Something special about each
person in our family

Someone our family admires
and talks about

A favorite story we tell in our family

Something we
like about where we live

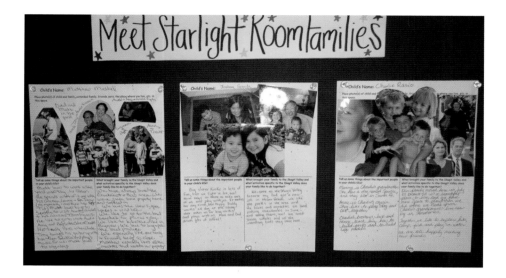

As the pages are brought to you, keep the family book in a prominent place where everyone can read it. Observe not only the information on the pages, but the way children talk about the information with each other. Notice if anything changes in the children's or families' conversations with one another. Does the family book give them a way to connect with one another? Does it serve as a springboard for more storytelling about family experiences?

As the year goes along, you can send home more pages to be filled out, asking for stories about such things as the day the child was born, birthday or holiday celebrations, or hopes and dreams the family has.

Invite Family Members to Share Stories of Their Childhoods

Inviting family members to come and tell the children a story about their own childhoods is a great way to learn more about who they are, and it furthers the bonds between the children and their own families. Stories about their families also create new interest and friendships between the children themselves.

Offer a general invitation, in writing, in person, and over the phone, to visit the classroom with a childhood story. Be sure to welcome extended family members and ask if they are willing to have their story written down and illustrated by you and the children so it can be preserved in a classroom book for ongoing enjoyment.

As family members visit, you get another opportunity to observe, hear, and support their connections with their child. Notice how your own relationship with them continues to deepen as well. When time permits, reflect on what you are learning, either in writing or with a coworker.

Child's Name _____   **Birthday** _____

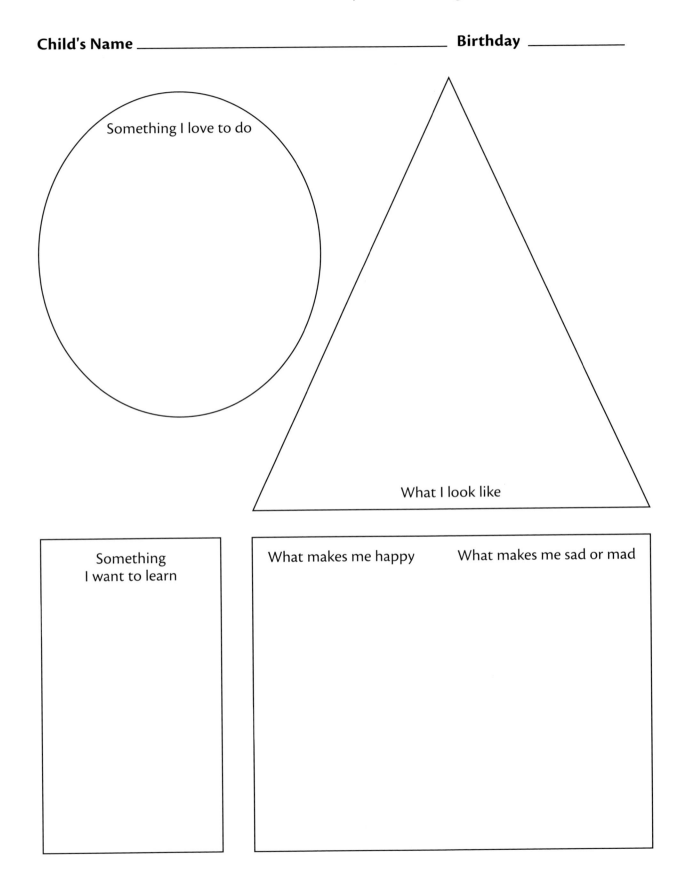

Something I love to do

What I look like

Something
I want to learn

What makes me happy   What makes me sad or mad

More Things to Do

As you develop strategies to involve and observe children with their families, remember to continue developing your own ability to see other perspectives.

Standing in Another's Shoes

To practice taking another person's perspective, try the following scenarios on your own or with a small group, and then reflect on what happened, using the questions that follow.

Situation: After a beautiful sunny morning, it begins raining really hard around noon. Act out the scene using the sentence "It's raining," from each of these perspectives.

- a farmer who has just finished planting seeds
- a school child who has been working in class all morning and has been looking forward to recess
- a weather reporter

Situation: A child discovers a large mud puddle on the playground and is splashing joyfully in it. Act out the scene and use the question "What are you doing?" from each of these perspectives.

- the teacher who is supervising the playground
- a parent who has come to pick the child up
- another child

The points of view and differences in the responses above are obvious, but how aware of this are you in your everyday work life? Continue exploring this idea by writing or sharing a story with a partner or small group about a time you had a completely different point of view from another person, even as you shared the same experience. Describe what happened and all of the possible perspectives of those involved.

Reflect on Another Quote

We all grow up with the weight of history on us. Our ancestors dwell in the attics of our brains as they do in the spiraling chains of knowledge hidden in every cell of our bodies.

—Shirley Abbott

Use these questions to help you reflect on the quotation from Shirley Abbott:

1   What does it mean to you?

2   How does it relate to your work with children?

Do some reflective writing or discuss this with others. Consider this example of two teachers' reflections on what it meant to them.

I had to read this several times before I knew how to think about it. The idea that we all carry our ancestors with us, whether we like it or not, can seem like either being blessed or cursed, depending on how mentally or physically healthy our families have been. Sometimes these are stories that we grow up with, but I was adopted, so I really don't know much about what I'm carrying from my birth family's genes. I often wonder about this. Am I like someone in my birth family who I'll never know or hear a story about? This quote reminds me to understand that each child who comes to us brings part of their family with them, whether or not we ever see those family members.—Hong-li, teacher

In one of my classes, our professor talked about children coming to school with "funds of knowledge" from their family. I'm guessing that's what Abbott means by "spiraling chains of knowledge" from our families being in our brains. Our professor reminded us how important it is to learn the strengths and family traditions of each child who comes to be in our program. This is especially important if they are living with the challenges of things like poverty, being uprooted as a refugee, or are less familiar with the expectations of our school system. We shouldn't see them as deficient, but rather as having their own strengths and know-how that we should try to understand. I guess I should also be thinking about the spiraling chains of knowledge I'm living with, which I haven't honestly considered.—Eleanor, family child care provider

Share Memories of "How We Did It"

To explore your own values and how they might be different from the families you work with, try this activity. In writing or with a partner or small group, describe how something was done in your family in areas such as health care, meal preparation, or discipline. As you compare your experiences with others in your group, see if this gives you insight into the different approaches families in your program may be taking in these areas.

Explore Cultural Traditions and Rituals

Find a selection of picture books that feature cultural traditions and rituals that welcome new babies into the family and community. Some suggestions are listed below. As you read these books, imagine the experience from the baby's point of view. Are there customs that intrigue you that could be adapted to welcome babies into your program?

> *Welcoming Babies* by Margy Burns Knight
> *Welcome Song for Baby* by Richard Van Camp
> *Welcome to the World* by Nikki Siegen-Smith
> *On the Day I Was Born* by Debbi Chocolate

Sample Observation Display

Read Lisa's story on the next page. Notice how thoughtfully she built on what she already knew about this child's family to investigate how his connection to his family and culture was developing. In sharing the story with the child's family, she was able to add their response to her final documentation display.

Kiaayo Knows His Culture

Kiaayo, I had the opportunity to share some of your family's music with you today. As I turned on the CD, you were playing at the table. How quickly you noticed and cocked your head to one side. In the next instant, you were off your chair and headed to the source of the sound. An expression of wonder was on your face while your mouth was rounded, making a happy little sound.

I could tell from what followed that this was familiar music to you, Kiaayo. You pointed to the music and then beckoned the other children by pointing at them and then back to the source music. Your enthusiasm for what you were hearing encouraged a group of children to come. The teachers soon saw that this could be a wonderful creative movement, so we added a large drum. We wanted to see what this would inspire the group to do.

Kiaayo, this event brought out your personality and qualities of leadership. While many babies circled the instrument, you moved forward and began to tap the instrument. You showed the others that it was safe to touch and how

it was to be used. The expression on your face illuminated the activity. I observed your head nodding to the beat and your body making many dance movements.

In the past, I have seen you take the feathers from our shelf and explore them. I often wondered if you had experience with feathers prior to the ones in the room. Today you again brought feathers from the shelf and tickled them on your face. Were you trying to teach us something? You brought the feathers to the drum and placed them on top.

We teachers decided to put video of native dancing on the laptop. Kiaayo, you watched with an intent look, and then I was thrilled to hear you shout, "Mommy, Daddy!" You pointed and repeated the words. This was the first time I had heard words from you. I was so proud! Kiaayo, you have moved into a phase of independence and social growth. Today you were able to demonstrate your prior knowledge and share it with us. You are now confident in attracting a group of children to join in your play.

I will continue to offer opportunities to explore your culture. We will listen to your music and play and experience a variety of drums. We also will learn with you as your language develops. Practicing Cree words along with English will help us communicate verbally. Embracing your culture will help you in expressing yourself.

—LISA, TEACHER

And here is the response from Kiaayo's family.

Dear Daycare Friends,

I was brought to tears by the letter Kiaayo brought home the day we sent him in with his powwow tunes. I was so proud of him. In our traditions, children are treated with great respect and honor because they are our future leaders. But as one youth said, "Youth are tomorrow's leaders, if we procrastinate!" Kiaayo has proven this to be true. He is already a leader. He was sharing and teaching his culture by showing the other children how to use the drum and how to dance. The drumbeat is the heartbeat of the earth and of our people. It is the first sound we hear in the womb. The drum brings families and communities together to celebrate, dance, socialize, pray, feast, and learn. He was sharing this with you when he brought everyone to the drum and brought the feathers to the drum.

I often tickle Kiaayo's face with the feathers that are part of my outfit. It was so sweet that he remembered this and was showing you all.

I was overjoyed that he is already learning so much about his culture and identity. We were at a traditional powwow this weekend, and Kiaayo was dancing with me and drumming with Lowell. It means so much to me that his identity and culture are validated and reinforced by his caregivers and friends. This will help him maintain balance in all parts of his life—spiritually, physically, mentally, and emotionally—which also represents the medicine wheel. The spirit is the essence of who we are as individuals. This includes our culture, identity, ceremony, and prayer. It is our belief that we need to balance all aspects of our life in order to be productive and peaceful individuals.

Hiy hiy, thank you. We look forward to coming to share more of our culture with you as the weather gets warmer.

—SANDRA AND LOWELL

Chapter 12

Getting Organized to Observe and Study Your Documentation

Through close observation of and personal relationship with each child and with the life of the classroom, one develops a sense of which moments to try to capture. Because I know, for example, that Elise has been engaging mostly in solitary play, I will take special note when she offers a spare Lego piece to Frank. Or because I know that Toshi and Jami have been talking endlessly about huge giants, I will take a picture when they begin to build tall block structures together. The observing and recording that a teacher does in an emergent context is not based on developmental checklists or assessment portfolios—it is a manifestation of her active engagement with the life of the program and with the children.—SARAH FELSTINER

As a teacher, nourishing your disposition and skills for observation is vital to enjoying and being successful in your job. With this foundation, you will come to appreciate who children are and find yourself eager to awaken others to the contribution these young ones can make to our lives. Your observations will become an essential source for enriching your environment and planning your curriculum. As you adopt the mind-set of a curious researcher, your observation practices will enhance your own professional development. In addition, they will give the children's families new insights into their children's capabilities. But none of this will come to pass without some planning and using tools to make the gathering and sharing of observation stories efficient and effective. You will need to get organized in order for teacher research and child-centered planning to become central to your work as a teacher.

Organizing systems will vary from person to person and program to program, according to your individual style, program expectations, and working conditions. You will want to consider your own preferences, your work environment, and the tools and technology you have available. This chapter summarizes ways to get yourself and your program organized for the documentation process. With this organization in place, we offer schema for studying your documentation. These will help you uncover and communicate possible meanings for what you are seeing so that you can decide what you might do next. When you get yourself organized, each observation you make

holds the promise of deepening your relationships with the children and their families and deepening your own understandings of the teaching and learning process.

Adopt a Method That Suits Your Style

The most important thing is to get started. Begin observing the children you work with. Choose a way of taking notes that suits your personal style as a teacher. For example, if you are not a particularly methodical person, you might start your observing practice in one of several ways:

- Put paper or sticky notes with pens in containers that are easy to reach all around your room. Some teachers find it helpful to wear an apron with a front pocket containing these things.

- Keep a simple spiral notebook handy with a pen attached.

- If you have easy access to technology, you may use these tools to help you gather documentation: still and video cameras, tablets, mobile devices, notebook computers, and laptops.

When you set yourself up with easy-to-access tools, you will have taken the first step toward documenting what you see and hear.

Once you begin regularly engaging in gathering documentation, you will then need a system for organizing the data you collect. Some teachers set up individual folders or journals for each child and drop their notes into these, either on paper or electronically. This works well for observing individual children, but you will also need a system for filing observations that include groups of children. Many teachers create files for group activities and then drop copies of that documentation into the individual folders for each child involved. However you choose to handle this, the goal is to have a system for tracking observations of individual children as well as capturing interactions between children, their conversations, conflicts, or growing common interests. This will enable you to discover their patterns, passions, and possible new materials to offer or curriculum projects to pursue.

Practice with Focused Observations

Because each day with a group of children offers many possibilities for capturing documentation, it is sometimes hard to choose what to take the time to record. With the ease of digital photography, many teachers start their documentation process by taking photos and using them to jog their memory about a particular experience they wanted to capture. Snapping a photo is so easy, so you must be careful not to take more photos than are useful in enhancing your understanding of children's endeavors. Whether you use pen and paper or a camera, you should have some values and goals to guide your decision about what moments to capture. These might include the following:

- Offering a glimpse into how children show us their unique perspectives.

- Providing a moment to show back to children the details of their actions, skills, and ideas.

- Recognizing a child's competency, even in the context of challenging behavior.

- Spotting a developmental leap, new insight, skill, or behavior in a child or group functioning.

- Capturing an example of children working within early childhood schema or a learning domain.

- Demonstrating children's work over time with particular materials, making connections, exploring theories, taking on challenges.

- Seeing something that answers or confirms something you have been curious or wondering about.

Having a research question of your own or one you have shared with other teachers is another way to focus your documentation process. You could formulate your research based on something you value, such as "How do girls and boys use the play yard differently?" or you could draw upon any of the study sessions in chapters 5–11 of this book. For instance, your research question might include:

- How are children using their senses to learn about something in our room or outdoors?

- What examples do we see of children using materials in our room to invent and construct?

- Where do we see examples of children's flexible thinking and focused study?

- Where do we see children demonstrating a connection to the natural world?

- How are children expressing a sense of power and adventure in their dramas?

- How are children using drawing or other materials to express their ideas? or What evidence do we have that children understand some aspects of literacy?

- How do children show us they are trying to negotiate a friendship?

- What examples do we see of children expressing a cultural identity or some aspect of life in their family?

If you are new to gathering observations, you may find it helpful to use a form to guide you. If you want to use forms, consider inventing ones that focus on the broad topics of the earlier study sessions of this book. Doing so will keep you alert to the details of children's actions and conversations and allow you to draw on your notes to explore the meaning of what you observed. Here are some simple examples of observation forms based on the themes explored in this book.

Topic: Friendships and Conflicts   Date _____/_____/_____   Time _____

Observed/Heard: _____

_____

Significance of this event: _____

_____

What skills and competencies did children use in this situation? _____

_____

Topic: Power and Adventure   Date _____/_____/_____   Time _____

Observed/Heard: _____

_____

Significance of this event: _____

_____

What skills and competencies did children use in this situation? _____

_____

Topic: Literacy and Symbolic Representation   Date _____/_____/_____   Time _____

Observed/Heard: _____

_____

Significance of this event: _____

_____

What skills and competencies did children use in this situation? _____

_____

Another focus for your research could be how children are using your room arrangements and the materials you are mandated to have on a Quality Rating and Improvement Systems (QRIS) rating scale. Rather than just mindlessly provisioning your classroom according to requirements, use these requirements to practice the art of awareness while assessing the value of these requirements. Focused observations on required room arrangements and materials might include questions like the following:

- How do we see children making use of the labels on our shelves for things like spatial awareness, one-to-one correspondence, classifying, or literacy?

- Do we see evidence that children are drawn to our multicultural materials in a way that strengthens their cultural identity?

- How are our caregiving routines supporting children's self-help skills?

Whatever your preference, choose an initial system that will get you right into the process of observation and organizing your data. Over time, you may want to refine or change things, but the goal is to get started and overcome any initial barriers. If you work in a program that has specific forms or paperwork systems required for assessments or accountability, your challenge is to reduce, not expand, any duplication of effort. You will have to experiment with how to integrate your everyday documentation approach into your requirements. If you do this well, you will have authentic evidence of meeting the desired outcomes for early learning that can be included in any required assessment tools.

The Rhythm of Observing

The typical early childhood teacher is responsible for a large group of children, along with many housekeeping and record-keeping tasks. If you think that collecting observations will require a large block of time to just sit and watch, weeks will slip by without you recording anything. Yet when you take five to ten minutes to jot down something you saw or heard because it delighted or irritated you, provoked your curiosity, or seemed significant to a research question, you will soon find yourself with a collection of small observations that can be strung together, like beads on a string.

The idea of seeing observations as beads on a string comes from college teacher Elizabeth Prescott. She uses the metaphor of beads to stand for children's activities, with the spaces between representing transitions. You can also think of the spaces between these beads as the passage of time. If you approach the observation process with this metaphor of collecting beads on a string, you will find a rhythm that looks like this: as you move about the room, you notice when a child or group of children begins to play or engage in something that is likely to last for a while. Jotting down some details and taking some photos is a potential bead for your string. When the activity ends or the children start to shift their attention to other things, this is a stopping place for this particular observation, a space on the string. Over time, as you continue this process and look over the notes and photos you have collected, you will notice which beads make sense to string together to tell a story of what has been going on with this child or group of children.

In teaching you how to record what you see, most observation textbooks make distinctions about a number of techniques:

- running records
- time samplings
- event samplings
- checklists
- anecdotal records
- diary or journal descriptions
- portfolio entries

The typical teacher rarely has time to employ all of these techniques. Prescott suggests trying an adaptation of running records, using lined paper and describing each new action of a child on a separate line. This enables you to notice closely, while quickly writing words or phrases. In the busy life of a classroom, you will probably want to invent word abbreviations for yourself. Whether you use a clipboard with lined paper, a form, a small sticky-note pad, or electronic device, the point is to jot down enough details to jog your memory when you find time to return to complete anecdotal information. With practice, you will begin to develop a rhythm for yourself, knowing when to just watch and not write, and when to lower your eyes and concentrate on a moment of writing.

Choose Your Technology

Because technology is advancing so rapidly, it's natural to use these tools to support your work as a teacher-researcher. Using technology is a powerful tool for documenting. Every day there are new options to consider, and you have to find what works best for you, your working conditions, and your budget. Video and still cameras will no doubt be your first tools for documenting, but be sure to use note taking to fill in the gaps. Putting a camera between you and children might actually interfere with what is unfolding, especially if they are tempted to stop and pose for you. Establish a guideline with the children that you only take pictures of children who are engaged in exploration, not posing for the camera. You can also invite them to join you in documenting their learning processes by showing them the photos as you take them. You can even offer the children a camera to take photos of what they think is important about what they've done. Sometimes a simple line drawing of what is unfolding will help you capture the process they are engaged in, which is ultimately more important than a final product.

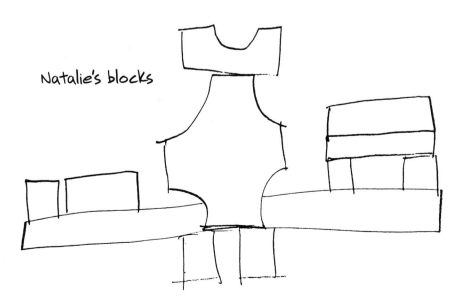

Natalie's blocks

A number of the children are experimenting with asymmetry. Natalie built this structure out of unit blocks. She added some blocks as I drew it to see if the structure would stay balanced.

There are some occasions, such as a focused group time, when an audio recording will help you capture conversation that goes by faster than you can write it down. This doesn't oblige you to transcribe everything you record. Rather, it serves as a backup for your documentation process and gives you the option of listening or transcribing to meet your needs. As a teacher new to observing and documenting, you may find audio recordings a valuable addition to your own eyes and ears. Comparing the recordings with your notes or memory can help you identify things you missed. Recordings from your classroom can become your teacher.

Consider Your Work Environment

Hand in hand with considerations of your own personal style are considerations of your work environment. Are you teaching alone or as part of a team? Do you have paid planning time that can be used for analyzing and developing stories from your observation data? Are there resources and support to help you with any language or cross-cultural aspects of understanding the meaning of your observations? Do you have a work space and the tools you need to study your documentation and choose some for posting as an observation display? Programs vary greatly in these areas. To teach with the pedagogy this book encourages, the ideal working conditions include:

- paid time and work station to study your documentation
- opportunities for collaborative discussions with other teachers

- resources on child development and the specific cultural and linguistic makeup of children and their families

- basic technology, including a digital camera, computer, printer, scanner, and copy machine

- a budget for ongoing upgrading of technology, software, and consumables like paper and ink

- basic training on the use of helpful technology, the elements of visual design, and any writing or second language skills you need to improve

If you looked at that list and panicked, fear not. Don't let the lack of something on the list keep you from beginning to observe the children you work with. Everything on this list is achievable, even if not at the moment. Together with your coworkers and director, you can begin to prioritize these as goals for your program. If your program is a nonprofit, grants can be written for most of the items on this list. Most programs have parents who are willing to donate small things, and some have employers or connections to resources that would be willing to donate to technology and training. You can put out a request for ideas on many of the online early childhood discussion groups. Find examples of how other programs have scheduled time for collaboration and working on documentation. Here are some suggestions from teacher Ann Pelo.

If you teach alone:

- Find another teacher in your program to be your observation partner. Try to spend time in each other's classrooms. For example, while your kids are in music class, you can visit each other's classrooms. Whether or not you spend time in each other's rooms, you can share notes, sketches, and photos of children and talk together about the children's growth and learning.

- Invite parents to spend time in your classroom. You can ask a parent to be available to children when they need help so you can spend some time observing, or you can ask a parent to observe and take notes for you while you work with children. If you ask parents to spend time observing, it's helpful to be specific about what you'd like the focus of their observations to be.

- On a bulletin board in the teacher lounge or in the office, post some notes that you took while observing kids, and ask other teachers to jot down their thoughts and insights about what you observed. You can also share documentation online through programs such as Google Docs.

- Include time on the agenda of staff meetings to talk about observations of children. Teachers on your staff can take turns bringing notes, sketches, or photos to the staff meeting for teachers to discuss together.

If you teach in a team:

- Schedule some time each week with your coteacher when one of you will spend time observing children while the other keeps track of general classroom activity.

- Develop cues to use with each other that signal that "I want to step out of the action and watch this play for a few minutes." Be sure to wait for an okay from your coteacher before you move into observation mode.

- Schedule a regular time to talk with your coteacher about your observations. Some teachers use naptime to talk together; others set up regular meetings with their coteachers about what they observe.

Getting started

- Schedule fifteen minutes for observation at a time during the day when the children are typically engaged in play. Write it on your daily schedule to honor your plan to observe children.

- Choose one area of the room to observe. What are kids doing in the block area? How are they using playdough?

- Focus on a particular child; watch and listen to her play, taking notes and photos.

- Pose a question that you are curious about, and pursue that question with observations. "How do children use books in my classroom?" "Do girls and boys use the blocks in different or similar ways?" "What role does Keiko, our youngest child, play in our group?"

However basic or advanced your experience, skills, and tools are, keep in mind that they are only a means to making your observations easily accessible, not an end in themselves. Your personal working style and program considerations will determine the best documentation system for you, while you strive to be as cost- and time-efficient as possible. Once you have developed a method of gathering observation notes and related visuals, your task will be to study your observation as carefully as you would any good resource for your learning.

Study to Find and Share the Important Story

Documentation cannot only capture the details of significant events and learning for the children but can also serve as a source of rich learning for teachers. Observation notes, sketches, and photos should not be viewed as something to quickly print up and put on display. Instead, first and foremost, you should comb through documentation with a curious mind, looking for surprises as well as evidence to substantiate hunches you might have made.

As you look over the notes, photos, and other traces of the children's

activities you've gathered, consider whether you see connections between this current work and other observations you've studied. If you've created a good, organized system of paper or electronic files, you can revisit those observations related to the same children or theme the children have explored in the past. For example, you can look in files of individual children or in folders with topics such as block play, dinosaurs, birthdays, or negotiating friendships. Perhaps your current observation reveals something you haven't seen before and represents a new stage of development for a child. Or maybe it's a new emerging interest among the children that could be nurtured along. (This could prompt you to set up a new folder based on that topic.)

Consider the Story from Different Perspectives

Typically observations are used to focus on some aspect of the learning or development seen in a child's activity. While this is valuable, it is only one of

the possible perspectives or stories worth considering. If you truly want to be child centered, you should consider children's perspectives—what was happening from their point of view—when studying your observations. This requires looking closely at the details you've captured and trying to discover how the children might be experiencing it. Questions to help you find this perspective are listed in the Four Perspectives to Consider chart on the next page.

Evidence of learning and development is often the story teachers, parents, and program monitors are typically seeking to find in documentation. The lens you bring to examining your observations for this purpose can be superficial or in-depth. It depends on your knowledge of child development, learning domains, early childhood learning theories, and knowledge valued from different cultural perspectives. You'll find questions to help you deepen your analysis of children's development and learning in the Four Perspectives to Consider chart.

As the teacher, you have a perspective that is important to consider as you study your documentation. Why did you take the time to capture this particu-

lar observation for study? What assumptions, curiosities, or hunches come to mind as you review your notes, photos, or work samples? In the teacher's story column in the chart, you'll find questions to help you discover your own perspectives on what this observation means to you.

Finally, you should always consider the family's story as a perspective that will help you think more deeply about your observations. Seeking their point of view about what you've seen will not only provide an opportunity for deeper insights but also strengthen your relationship with the child and family members.

Four Perspectives to Consider

THE CHILD'S STORY	THE LEARNING AND DEVELOPMENT STORY	THE TEACHER'S STORY	THE FAMILY'S STORY
• What is the child doing with the materials?	• How does this activity relate to things you've seen before?	• What were you curious about as you watched and listened?	• How might this play reflect or challenge the child's family's beliefs, values, or practices?
• How does the child's tone of voice suggest what seems engaging to this child? Body language? Facial expressions? Hand gestures?	• What knowledge, skills, or theories do you see the child expressing?	• What delighted or surprised you?	• What might the family find meaningful about this activity?
• How does the child talk about and represent thinking in the play?	• What new ideas, questions, understandings, or solutions is the child discovering?	• What do you want to learn more about?	• How could dialogue about this observation strengthen your relationship with the family?
• What other experiences, people, and materials does the child connect this experience with?	• Is there any confusion, contradiction, stereotype, or misinformation coming out in this activity?	• How do you relate this observation to what you value and see as the child's competency?	• How will you seek out the perspective of the child's family and learn their ideas about possible next steps?
• What is the child inventing and investigating through this play or activity?	• How is this experience supporting or undermining a positive sense of identity for this child?	• What hunches do you have about the meaning of this activity for this child?	
• Do the child's actions and words suggest how the child's individual or group identity is evolving?	• Does this activity reveal the child's self-regulation or learning disposition? Why or why not?	• How does what you see help you learn more about the teaching and learning process and how you can better support the child?	
	• What early childhood schema theory do you see at work in this child's activity?	• What are some possibilities for next steps you might take to extend or deepen this play or to challenge the child's thinking?	
	• How is this child working with ideas related to learning domains such as the following: —language/literacy development —creative/ representational arts —scientific thinking/ inquiry —mathematics —antibias/ critical thinking —physical science		

As you study the observations and documentation collections you gather, you can explore each of these perspectives as a possible perspective or story to expand your thinking. The following examples of observation notes demonstrate how this study process might work, whether you are studying your observations on your own, with your teaching team, or even in a conference with the children's parents. Study how the teachers use the Four Perspectives table to reflect on the following examples of observation notes.

10:10 am Luke goes to sit with Ms Yvonne, our visiting teacher. He rolls playdough in little balls. Starts singing the "Muffin Man" as takes rolled balls, presses flat, pounds on them. Picks up pizza cutter and starts cutting flattened balls.

10:17 am. Ms. Montoya brings muffin pan and puts in front of Luke. He places muffins in the pan . . . counting 1, 2, 3. Sees Ms Yvonne taking his picture. Moves closer to her, laying head on her shoulder. Ms Yvonne shows him picture of muffins on the table. He immediately takes the muffins and smashes them on table. Begins to makes lines on the flat playdough, saying "railroad tracks". Goes again to look at new photo on camera screen.

10:25 am Luke gives Ms Yvonne some playdough and says, "take a picture". When he sees zoom lens move toward him, his eyes light up . . . Says, "Again" during the game.

Luke's interaction with this visitor went on for more than twenty minutes.

THE CHILD'S STORY

- Is it the visitor or the playdough that draws Luke to the table?
- Seems to enjoy feel of playdough as it rolls and when he smashes it.
- Connects playdough balls with idea of muffins and song he knows and seems to like.
- Drawn to camera and at ease with Ms. Yvonne; seems to feel safe and willing to engage with stranger.
- Invents a game that seems to delight him and keep his focus.
- Wants to express his understanding with words he knows.

THE LEARNING AND DEVELOPMENT STORY

- Remembers song related to shape of muffins.
- Confident to approach stranger and include physical contact.
- Fine-motor skills for rolling.
- Exploring cause and effect—knows pounding will flatten playdough.
- Recognizes his work on camera screen and uses that to revisit and do more with playdough.
- Knows that railroad tracks are made with lines (schema theory?).
- Initiates social invitation into a game with body and words.
- Attaches words to his understanding of the zoom lens.
- Extended focus for more than twenty minutes.
- Several milestones here with communication, social engagement, and focused attention over time.

THE TEACHER'S STORY

- So pleased to see Luke's social initiation and willingness to lean close to stranger.
- Did his interest in the playdough and camera help mediate his comfort level?
- Curious about whether he saw things I didn't in looking between camera screen and playdough muffins.
- What prompted drawing lines? Did he intend to represent railroad tracks or only make that connection when he saw the lines?
- Can we offer him more opportunities with a camera, perhaps eventually as a tool to use on his own? Will that prompt more communication and social engagement?
- Want to find other "zoom-related" materials to see if he will transfer interest and initiate the game again.

THE FAMILY'S STORY

- Questions to explore with the family:
  —Have you seen Luke start to show more comfort with strangers like we did today?
  —We wonder if you have been doing extra work with Luke on using language or if we are just witnessing a milestone for a new level of communication on his part.
  —How might we work together to support his interest in cameras and creating a game that evokes more communication and social engagement?
  —Would you like to see a shift in his IEP, or shall we continue to work on the current objectives?

2/17 Rebecca walked around the room gathering things to put in her basket—block, stuffed animal, book, beads, and toy car. Then she began giving these things to children she encountered. With only car left in her basket, she headed over to the window into the infant room where Kai had pulled himself up and was looking in. Rebecca sat down and put the toy car on the window ledge which immediately captured Kai's attention. Making motor-like sounds "rhmmm, rhmmm," Rebecca began zooming the car up the window. Kai's eyes followed the car and a smile broke out on his face. He seemed delighted with what he saw.

Observation Study Benefits Both You and the Children

Rather than rushing to print photos and post your observation notes, first take the time to study what you see as the significance of the activity. Use your photographs as another set of eyes and any audio recordings as a way to revisit both the context and details of the observation.

When you consider possible meaning from different points of view, you develop a flexible mind; you avoid assuming there is only one possible interpretation or story. Seeking multiple perspectives will expand your examination and help you become a more critical thinker.

THE CHILD'S STORY	THE LEARNING AND DEVELOPMENT STORY	THE TEACHER'S STORY	THE FAMILY'S STORY
• Confident at home and mobile in the room. • Basket seems important to hang on to, even though other things can be given away. • Is Rebecca seeking out playmates by offering them materials?	• Self-directed and engaged. • Creating opportunities for social relations. • Uses appropriate sounds for car. • Is she taking Kai's perspective as she invents the car game with him? • Was this a purposeful plan or just spontaneous actions?	• Delighted to see her ease in offering toys to other children; defies the notion that toddlers are self-centered and can't yet share. • Curious about whether she chose random objects or was selective about what she put in basket. • If we offered her more baskets, would she distribute them to others? • Use this photo to make a book about inviting friends to play. • Would she like to pursue a friendship with Kai or any of the other babies? Let's explore options. • Let's see if she shows any interest in dolls.	• Questions to explore with the children's families: —Does Rebecca spend time with babies at home? She seemed so able to figure out what would engage Kai and bring him delight. —We wonder if you involve her in helping with chores at home, because she seems so confident in taking up a task like distributing toys. —Does this observation seem consistent with what you see in your family?

Ideally teachers learn the most by studying their observations with others, but even when that's not possible, the Four Perspectives chart can serve as a framework to widen your considerations.

Once you've taken time to examine your documentation, you have a number of choices before you. The next chapter explores the many ways you can use your observations to benefit your ongoing learning and that of the children in your care.

Chapter 13

Using and Sharing Your Observations with Others

As we move around the circle of life, there are certain things we must do if we are to learn and grow and live a good life. The first step is to listen. If we do not listen, then we will hear nothing. The second step is to observe. If we do not look carefully at things, then we will not really see them. The third step is to remember. If we do not remember those things we have learned, then we have learned nothing. The fourth step is to share. If we do not share, then the circle does not continue. —JOSEPH BRUCHAC

Becoming an aware listener and observer will surely enhance your view of children. Approach the task of documenting as a process of collecting and telling the stories of their remarkable childhood experiences. In this way, you can influence how others view children as well. When teachers turn their observations into oral, written, and visual stories, children sense that their pursuits are worthy of being documented, described, and remembered. Their families, too, are rewarded with the details of what the children have been doing, thinking, and learning. Teachers get windows into how their colleagues think—what they find significant and meaningful. Sharing observation stories will make your job better, easier, and more fun.

Observations Can Enhance Your Disposition, Knowledge, and Planning

Heightening your awareness through close observation helps you remember what you value about being with children. You can reenter this precious time of life with a new approach, recognizing how brief it is and how much you gain from noticing the details of what is unfolding. Paying attention in this way nourishes you emotionally. It also enhances your intellectual curiosity and sparks your interest in finding out more about individual children and their development and learning processes.

What you see and hear in your daily observations will give you a wealth of ideas for planning a curriculum that is meaningful and relevant to the children's lives. You will find any number of seeds for growing desired learning outcomes. Sometimes these will become extended, in-depth curriculum projects, but often they are just ordinary moments that are reflections of the ongoing learning process children engage in.

Learn to Value Ordinary Moments

Once you tune in to the details of what children are doing and saying, you will often be astonished. These details will show you how children are growing and changing, expanding their interests and know-how in the smallest of gestures. As you come to value this, you will begin to feel each moment is important and worthy of recording, even the ones that seem ordinary at first glance. Of course, time and competing demands won't permit you to capture each moment in writing. You will need to make choices about what to preserve. Perhaps you will spot one of those many firsts or discover a pattern that a child is repeating again and again. Let these moments linger with you, and share them with others. They are the stuff of the moment, the lives of children in the here and now, not some anticipated future you might not witness.

Descriptions of ordinary moments can be presented to others as sound-bite stories, alerting readers to how extraordinary the ordinary lives of children are. Here are a few examples.

We've had the projector in our room all week, with a basket of things next to it for the children to explore light and shadow. Hayley took this a step further, going around the room and finding other things to try. She was excited when she put the menorah on the projector but puzzled when she didn't see its shadow projected on the wall. "Oh, I get it," she then announced, as she laid the menorah flat and watched its giant shadow appear on the wall. In that moment, we saw Hayley making connections with what she had learned in the past about how the projector lamp and mirrors would interact with objects placed on the glass.

—BETSY, TEACHER

Sara spent a good part of fifteen minutes today examining and manipulating the translucent colored building materials we offered on the floor in a basket. Look at her face and how she is carefully studying the two pieces she has in her hands. Time and time again she did this, often placing one on top of another and then looking up at us with a smile on her face as if to say, "Look what I'm figuring out." We wonder if she sees the color change with the blocks placed this way or if she is pleased with her coordination, so carefully, which lines up the two blocks. Whatever is on her mind, she reminds us that it's so wrong to characterize babies as having no attention span.   —MARGIE, TEACHER

We observed Jonah watching others use this gooey mixture as they learned to make paper. When asked if he wanted to do it, Jonah replied, "I don't want to touch it." We wondered aloud if there was a way for him to explore the making of paper without having to touch the gooey mixture. He said, "I know. I can use gloves!" We are so pleased with the way Jonah is inventing ways to take up things that are challenging for him. Even though the gloves weren't sized for his hands, you can see by the look on his face that he was determined to make this work.   —VICKY, TEACHER

See Yourself as a Researcher and Learner

Use your observations to enhance your own learning as well as the children's. When you see children's keen eyes noticing everything around them, you can use the child's attention to stimulate your own disposition toward being attentive. When you observe a gesture of kindness a child makes toward someone who is upset, you can use it as inspiration to enrich your own empathy. As you watch and listen carefully to children's activities, you will see child development principles and early learning theories in action. Or perhaps you will see something that calls these theories into question, such as Piaget's notion that young children are egocentric and can't yet take the perspective of another. Being an astute observer gives you the opportunity to see examples of progress in different learning domains when children demonstrate skills referred to as *scientific thinking*, *math concepts*, and *self-regulation*.

You may encounter children who teach you to take another look because their competency isn't the first thing you notice. Sometimes things about children's behaviors feel like a disappointment rather than a gift. They can irritate rather than delight you. These are the moments to practice the art of reframing—to seek the children's point of view rather than yield to the temptation to label, if not punish, children. A more productive approach is to try to transform an irritation into something you are curious about, asking yourself questions like these:

- Why is this happening?
- What do I need to see that I don't yet understand?
- What is the underlying source and meaning of this behavior?
- What story might this child be trying to tell us?

If you view irritating behaviors as unfolding stories you don't yet understand, your emotional reaction and the way you proceed with the children will likely shift. If you see yourself as a researcher trying to find the meaning of particular play or conversation themes, your focus for observing will be sharper. Your stories about what you are seeing and hearing can draw others into the process. This can help create a collaborative project for teacher self-development and curriculum planning, along with more focused conversations with parents.

Sample Teacher Research Study

All week, a group of boys in the block area have been enthusiastically focused on creating ramps for their cars. Their play is very active and loud, especially when they line up blocks to crash into at the bottom of the ramp, creating a domino effect. Teachers Deb and Rhonda feel conflicted about how

to respond. They are annoyed by this play and really don't like the noise level in the room. Still, they ask themselves, when no one is getting hurt and the children seem very involved in the play, should it be stopped just because it's loud and irritating to us?

Because they aren't sure of the value of this play and whether they should allow it to continue, Deb and Rhonda decide to adopt the role of researchers. They watch and listen closely to this noisy play, taking notes and drawing sketches.

One day, after the children have gone home, Deb and Rhonda go to the block area and use their documentation to recreate the children's ramp structures and begin imitating the loud car crashing play. To their surprise, they discover how exciting it is to adjust the ramp so the cars go faster and to experiment with how to place the blocks at the ramp's end to create a crashing domino effect. They also find that it takes careful planning and placement to position the ramp and the blocks to create the domino effect. Through their research, they not only receive insight into the emotional thrill involved but also discover what good engineers the children are.

With a better understanding of the value of this loud, active play, the next day they return to the children with a plan to provide more space and opportunity. Rather than outlawing this loud, annoying play, Rhonda and Deb develop provocative questions for the children and additional materials to explore cause and effect, speed and velocity for this chain-reaction effect that is so exciting. This might not have happened had they not explored the materials themselves, trying to understand what the children find so enjoyable about this exuberant play.

Use Your Observations to Invite Reflection and Dialogue

Your documentation not only serves as an accountability system for your teaching; it also has great potential to contribute to the formation of strong partnerships with coworkers and families. We all know that working closely with parents is emphasized in early childhood professional literature. Yet our busy lives and potential communication barriers often leave the ideal of partnerships a vague abstraction or an unmet goal.

Partnerships develop over time and most effectively occur when there is mutual respect and a specific, mutual focus. Be generous with your observations when talking with families. Reveal how you value the details of what the children are doing and how carefully you think through your planning for them. Families will be eager to add their knowledge and stay in close communication.

Early childhood educator Ann Pelo describes how she uses her observations with families in this way:

Stories, photos, and detailed notes invite families to join teachers in thinking about what's happening with their children. Working in full-day child care, I don't see parents every day. Actually, there are some parents whom I rarely see because our schedules don't intersect at all. But family members come to the classroom every day, whether I see them or not, and they look around and try to get glimpses of what their children are doing.

To provide windows into children's play and learning for families, I try to create bulletin board displays that reflect the evolving life of the children. I use photos and quotes from kids and examples of the work they are doing as a project unfolds. These windows invite families to look at children's play with curiosity and delight.

If I'm there when families are dropping off or picking up their children, I try to lure them over to a bulletin board, to point out details: "I took that photo when we first began using a wheelchair in our classroom. Kids noticed right away that our shelves were too low for them to reach if they sat in a wheelchair, and they began talking about how to make our classroom 'more fair.'"

Lately I've tried to include brief statements about my thinking in displays, so that even if I'm not there, I can talk with families. I might add a question that helped guide my planning or pose a question for viewers to consider. I might add tips for families to use as they study their children's work. I write things like:

"I wasn't sure how much the children understood about using a wheelchair. I took these notes while they took turns riding in a wheelchair, so I could learn more about what they understood."

"What are your goals for your child as she or he investigates accessibility issues and ramps?"

"Notice the different ways the children tried to draw the depth of a ramp. It's a challenge to move from three dimensions into two."

When teachers conscientiously design, post, or e-mail observation stories for families, they get more respect and involvement from them. This, in turn, begins to transform teachers' own attitudes and communications. You become more curious, less judgmental, and more willing to go that extra mile to make it possible for the children's families to be involved with what you are doing. Rather than viewing observations as another requirement, think of using them to enhance your own and the children's growth and the partnership you want to develop with their families.

Publicly sharing your observations can enhance your teamwork as a staff too. Often schedules in full-day children's programs make it difficult for the morning and afternoon staff to meet and plan together daily. You can post some observation notes, including your questions or thinking, and invite other teachers to add theirs. Even with minimal overlap in your schedules, this will help you work more closely with a similar focus. It is also a way to informally mentor new or less experienced teachers so they observe, think about, and communicate what they are seeing and hearing.

Because your observation stories are such an important tool for learning to collaborate, it makes sense to invent some systems to share with the children's families and your coworkers. Here are some strategies to try.

Alert Families

Designate a particular area of the room for posting things for families. Find at least three different ways to alert them to this posting—for instance, a note in newsletters, cubbies, or on the door; phone calls, e-mails, or a tour at drop-off or pickup time; or colorful paper footprints from the entryway to the board. Include a clipboard or notepad in your posting for getting immediate input from families.

Send Home an Observation Book

Develop a traveling notebook binder with observation notes and photos in plastic sleeves. Set up a checkout system for the book to go home with the children. Make its language child-friendly so it can become a family reading project. Include a blank page for families to add their responses to their reading.

You can, of course, do something similar digitally, but getting kids oriented toward printed books is important for their ongoing literacy development.

Create a Staff Observation Sharing System

Designate a place for sharing observations with your coworkers. Make sure it is set up for two-way communication. Agree on a system for keeping current with how you are making use of this. When you invent a system that works well for you, share it with other teachers—in your program, on blogs and websites, and in the profession at large through an Internet discussion group, a conference presentation, or articles in a professional newsletter, magazine, or journal.

As observation becomes the heart of your teaching, you will discover all the ways it can be used to enhance your goals and even inspire new ones. Mindful observing is a give-and-take cyclical process. You will also find great enjoyment and benefit in reading stories of other teachers who demonstrate the various ways you can practice being a teacher-researcher. Put your observations of children at the center of your thinking, storytelling, and advocacy to get the resources you need for this kind of work.

Sharing your observation stories in conversations or writing will give others a window into your thinking and invite a dialogue. This, in turn, will help strengthen your voice and agency as an early childhood educator. Toddler teacher Emily Viehauser sometimes focuses her observation stories on individual children and other times on group themes that seem to be emerging. In either case, her intent in sharing her stories is to strengthen her relationships with her coworkers and the children's families by offering them a story about something that captured her attention and a request to hear how others react to it. Here are two examples.

In the first story, Emily captures the thread of an ongoing theme in her toddlers' play. With some sample photos, she e-mails and posts documentation to invite the children's families to value their children's representations as expressions of symbolic thinking and to consider where their inspiration comes from.

Cakes

Kids have been making lots and lots of cakes lately. Sometimes it's a birthday cake and comes with a song attached. But what I've noticed the most is that a wide variety of materials are being used for their cakes. It makes me think about the idea that different materials speak differently to different people. While Isla sees the possibility for a cake with the Wedgit blocks, Bryce and Evan use the Wedgits to make towers. Jonah uses them to make tunnels. Isabelle sees sand as a good tool for representing cake, while Zev uses sand to make coffee and digs in with his feet. Playdough speaks to Danika and Myla about cakes, but Will uses playdough to make cookies. Sebastian sees the possibility to make airplanes in the dough.

It also brings up a question for me that I often wonder about, similar to the saying "Which comes first, the chicken or the egg?" I think about this idea in relation to the source of young children's inspiration. Are they first inspired to make a cake and *then* seek out the material that supports their idea? Or does their inspiration begin from the way a specific material speaks to them?

The conclusion I most often come to is that it works both ways, and depending upon the individual child, they may sway more one way than the other. Where do you think your child develops most of his or her inspiration?

—EMILY, TEACHER

The second example from Emily reflects on her observations and inter-actions with a bilingual child in her group. Her hypothesis is that he under-stands materials can be used as different languages for the same idea, just as he uses English and his home language of Portuguese. In this example, she is also using an adaptation of the Learning Story format from New Zealand dis-cussed in chapter 14.

Lucas's Towers

What happened: This morning Lucas was messing around with the Duplo blocks: pushing the already connected pieces off and picking up pieces from the basket and tossing them around. I wondered what he was working on. Making sounds? Creating chaos? Exploring destruction? Learning about cause and effect? I watched for a short time, and it all seemed a little haphazard, so I wondered if Lucas might be unsure about how to use the Duplo blocks. So I asked, "Lucas, should we make a tower?" "Make tower," he said. He watched as I showed him how to push the blocks onto the platform and onto

each other, and then he immediately began stacking them up in the form of a tower. I stepped away for a minute to help another child but was soon met with Lucas's hand in mine. He began to pull me through the room, saying, "Make tower, make tower." He led me toward the big wooden blocks and continued to say, "Make tower, make tower." Then he took the blocks one by one and began stacking

them up. He stacked two cubes on top of each other and added an arch to the very top. Then he said, "Tower, tower!"

What it means: After using the smaller muscles of his hands and fingers to make a tower out of Duplos, Lucas realized that he could also make a tower out of the big wooden blocks. He was excited to share with me that he had made a connection between two different building materials. I was especially impressed with this particular correlation because I have only seen Lucas interact more forcefully with the big wooden blocks by tossing them around and pushing them over. He seemed to realize that he could transform these blocks into something familiar.

Lucas also seems to be showing us that he can represent his ideas in multiple ways and with different mediums. I wondered, too, if this might be helpful to Lucas while he's learning about the English language. Perhaps this sort of representation parallels Lucas's language acquisition, symbolizing the idea that lots of words can mean the same thing.

Opportunities and possibilities: In the next few weeks, I'd like to follow Lucas around and suggest he make a tower with even more materials like playdough, puzzle pieces, or even cars. Ideally, I'd also like to put together a photo book of all the different towers he creates with this language of building so that he has a visual collection of the multiple ways to represent a tower.

Parent's response: We absolutely *loved* the story about Lucas and his towers! Towers are definitely a big passion of his and more specifically, *bell* towers. It started with a book in which he saw a bell, and from there he asked us for more "bell," so we showed him a few YouTube videos of bells, most of them associated with towers. He definitely associates them and sometimes calls "bell tower" an individual bell or any kind of tower. A popular outing on weekends is to go to Ballard and see their little bell tower. He always gets a mix of fear and excitement from the sound of the bell!

Even though it was prompted by us, one example I can think of making the same thing out of different materials was when we were drawing tractors with him with crayons, and then later we would make a tractor together out of playdough. He got very excited by that and would start to do the same in his own way. Sometimes he can also play with different things around the house that remotely resemble a bell, and he even makes the soundtrack (*clang, clang, clang*).

Lucas is always excited to share with us his discoveries, and one of them has definitely been the English learning. One of these days I said, "Let's wash our hands" in Portuguese, he repeated in English, and I got very excited and said, "That's right, that's how you say it in English," and he was all smiles! He also thinks it is fun when we teach him the names of objects in both Portuguese and English.

So I definitely think that he was excited to show you he could build the same thing out of different materials and that this relates to the language. I like this story so much because to me it also shows that he was just basically very excited to be able to communicate with you in English!

—RENATA

Use Your Observations with the Children Themselves

Documentation of observations doesn't have to be used only by adults. Children can be involved in the process as well. When you offer your observations back directly to the children, you promote a self-reflection process in them. You give them more language and the early experience of *metacognition*—thinking about their thinking process. This enables them to consider what else they might do and to gain experience in naming their intentions. Children's ability to describe more details about their undertakings will enhance their connections between the classroom and their home life. It will also expand their vocabulary, and a good vocabulary is a key predictor of school success.

Children benefit enormously from hearing your stories about them and seeing evidence of what they have been doing. This enhances their self-esteem and their connections with one another. One of the most immediate ways you can use your observations is to describe the details of what you see them doing right on the spot. If you have done any sketching or taken any photos, you can show those to the children, either right on the camera screen, your tablet, or a computer. Helping children see themselves and their lively minds is a great way to use your observations in a timely way. As children become accustomed to reviewing their work with you in this way, they can be offered a camera to begin capturing things they would like to put in their portfolios or revisit at a later date. You can purposefully offer children printed and assembled documentation for them to review and consider where their ideas might take them next.

Hearing observations of what they have been doing can stimulate children's learning. When they are vividly reminded of what they have been doing, it often stimulates children to go further with an idea, expanding or deepening their pursuits, and sometimes encountering the need for a cognitive or emotional leap. Early childhood educator Ann Pelo describes it this way:

As children reflect on their earlier play, as they revisit their work, they can think in new ways about their experiences. It's just like we adults hone our thinking by study and reflection over time. Children may have conversations with one another in which they use their earlier experiences as launching pads into new learning. They may decide to repeat an earlier experience to get it clear in their minds. They may tell the story of the experience to someone who was not involved.

"Hey, look at that photo! Remember when we made that rocket ship with blocks? Let's make it again!"

"What do those words say?"
"They say, 'Casey sorted the dinosaurs into two groups: a group of mommies and a group of daddies.'"
"Oh, yeah, I did that! I'm going to make more groups today: brothers and sisters."

"Why did you make that drawing?"
"Well, I wanted to show how I looked when I was dressed up like a princess. See, we were playing a game about a king and queen, and I wanted to join the game, but Tara said I had to be a princess. First, I didn't want to be. Then Stu found a crown for me to wear, and then I wanted to be the princess."

You can use your circle or meeting time to share stories about what you have seen them doing. Some of these can be put into little books, read to the children, and put in the book area to be read independently by the children. Sketches or photographs with sound-bite stories of your observations can be placed on bulletin boards, on room dividers, or in Plexiglas frames on shelves in the area where they took place. As this becomes a regular practice, the children will refer to this documentation to remind one another of what they have done or to remember how to approach a particular activity again. As a result, they continue to practice skills, expanding their vocabulary and their sense of belonging. They learn the meaning of reference books.

One of the best uses of whiteboards in the classroom is to use them with photos or videos that allow the children to immediately revisit what they have just been doing. As the children view this documentation of their activities, ask them if they would like to do anything more with this idea. Record their discussion about this possibility and bring it back to them the next day.

Writing Can Help You Find and Tell Stories

With a combination of photos, children's words or work samples, and detailed observation notes, you can often discover a story worth developing and telling. The challenge is to gain confidence as a writer so you can paint a picture with your words. Though there is a saying that a picture is worth a thousand words, you should use photographs to help you generate descriptive words, not as a substitute for them. The reader of your observation will benefit from hearing your lively description of what happened and what you think is significant about it. Consider the difference between a photo caption and a descriptive story accompanied by photos.

CAPTION	DESCRIPTIVE STORY
Everybody had fun at the pumpkin farm, especially Tina.	Once we arrived at the pumpkin farm, everyone burst onto the field, arms outstretched as if to embrace each ball of courage. Tina bent down closely to look at each one, perhaps picturing its soon-to-be face.

Here are some strategies to help you find the descriptive words to bring your story alive, with or without photos.

Practice Using Word Webs to Generate Descriptive Details

In chapter 9, you practiced an *Art of Awareness* activity in which you created a word web. You can use this simple strategy to begin to spin out words for your observation story. Put a single word or a photo in the center of a piece of paper and then draw out other words from this, particularly action verbs and sensory adjectives and adverbs that describe more about this idea. Make a goal of generating at least ten initial words. Then try to find three other words to spin off from each of the ten. Now you have the bones of a good story concept.

Choose the words that seem most appropriate and appealing to you, and begin to form them into short sentences. Soon you will have a few sentences as the foundation of a descriptive paragraph, like the simple descriptive story about the pumpkin farm. If you have actual quotes from the children, you can insert them into the narrative. These can be quotes collected while they were involved in the activity or when you showed them a photo of it.

Practice Collaborative Webbing and Writing

Working with others to develop stories is a great way to expand your perspectives as well as your descriptive vocabulary. Collaborative word webbing helps you mentor each other across your areas of strengths and through your learning goals. Some teachers become keen observers but are hesitant in their writing skills. Others find that words flow easily in oral storytelling, but they need a scribe to translate their ideas into writing. Before working on your observation notes together, try practicing this activity with another person.

1   One person is the storyteller, while the other is the scribe.

2   The storyteller begins by describing a favorite memory of a time while working with a child. Recall as many sensory details as possible. What was the time of year, the temperature of the day, the lighting, sounds, and smells? What specifically unfolded when you were together? Are there facial expressions, colors, or actions you can describe in detail?

3   While the storyteller is talking, the scribe creates a web of words and phrases from the story.

4   Before changing roles, the scribe may want to add some additional words that come to mind from the story, putting them on a different place on the web.

5   Change roles, with the scribe becoming the storyteller and the first storyteller becoming the scribe. Following the same guidelines, repeat the activity in your new roles.

6   When both people have told their stories, exchange the word webs so you each have words for your own story in front of you. Take these words and begin to write a paragraph of your story.

7   The next time you work together, you can practice with actual observation notes and photos of children in your care.

Practice Using the Four Perspectives to Consider

Look at the chart on page 221 to help you explore possible paragraphs you can develop to share your observation story. Remember to describe the unfolding process of the activity, not just the final outcome. Along with your observation notes, other pieces of data can help you fill in the details of a story you want to make visible. Sketches, photos, transcripts of audio or video recordings, examples of things children have made, and resources you have offered all serve to help you understand and then translate your observations into a meaningful story. After you describe what happened, consider questions that seek the child's perspective on this event. Add your own voice, and pose some questions seeking the family's input.

Sharing Observation Stories Integrates Learning

Because there are so many pressures and demands on teachers, it's easy to think of gathering observations as just another accountability system. But if you take the approach suggested in this book, you will quickly discover that the process begins to enhance your teaching in numerous ways. The act of becoming more mindful in your teaching keeps you in tune with how you are feeling, what you are thinking, and what's going on with the children. Your job will become more enjoyable, and you will become more intentional in your planning and in responding to children. Relationships are strengthened through sharing observation stories. Curriculum ideas begin to flow from what's actually meaningful to the children. The children's learning becomes more integrated, and so does yours.

Chapter 14

Using Observations for Planning and Assessment

Observation can be used not only as the basis of information about individual children and the building of a classroom community, but also as the place from which teachers can begin to engage in the dialogic process of reflection, hypothesis building, and planning.
—GRETCHEN REYNOLDS AND ELIZABETH JONES

Planning curriculum and assessing children's learning are key responsibilities of an early childhood educator. But increasingly these activities are taking on the appearance of elementary school teaching, where lesson plans are geared toward a set of expected outcomes for children. This is otherwise known as *teaching to the test*. Early childhood teachers who embrace what our profession calls *developmentally appropriate practice* take a different approach. We put thoughtful attention into planning an engaging environment and then observing how children use it. Teaching goals are then integrated into plans that respond to the children's interests and pursuits. Likewise, when we want to introduce content topics, child-centered teachers offer the children some introductory-related materials and conversations. And then we stay alert to discover what the children already know about the topic and what their experiences and theories are. From those reflections, we plan a scaffold to move the children's learning to a new set of understandings. The focus is on learning rather than teaching.

Studying your observation notes with your teaching team can become one of the most valuable resources you have for individual and group curriculum planning. Rather than arbitrarily choosing a theme for planning curriculum activities, first consider what you have been seeing and hearing as the children

play. As a starting place, use the questions below with some photos or observation notes you have on hand. Practice identifying what seems most engaging to the children and how that might be further supported in your planning. As you become more experienced, you can study your documentation with the Four Perspectives to Consider chart introduced in chapter 12 on page 221.

- What is the essence of this experience from the child's point of view?
- What does this child know and know how to do?
- What is this child exploring, experimenting with, or trying to figure out?
- How does this observation reveal the child's self-concept or emerging identity?
- Do you see a place where the child can benefit from some coaching, questioning, or additional materials to take the activity to a more complex level?
- What values and learning goals do you want to influence the response you make?

When you plan for individual children, you can study your observation notes for play themes. In addition, look for social, emotional, and cognitive patterns or schema. Making children's interests and strengths the springboard of your planning will move you away from the prevailing deficit model of individualizing. It will help children's families know that you are seeing fully and not just looking for possible problems or areas needing improvement.

Provide a Window into Your Planning Process

When you include your own thinking about curriculum planning in the written documentation you post, you help others see how you approach planning from your observations. For those looking for a preplanned or school-readiness curriculum, this provides reassurance. It is also an important measure of your accountability to plan outcomes for the children's learning. For example, preschool teacher Sarah Felstiner shares her thinking by publicly posting an analysis of some observation notes next to some photos, conversation transcripts, and examples of the children's activities. Note how she thinks aloud for her own and other adults' benefit. She makes clear what her curriculum plans are. She demonstrates accountability in a way that is ultimately more meaningful than putting names of activities in little boxes on a lesson plan schedule.

November 4

Looking back at these snippets of children's experiences over the past few months, I begin to see possibilities for an extended project around the ideas of hiding and trickery, ships and the *Titanic*, sparkly things and treasure. Until now I've been watching and waiting, focusing the curriculum around group identity and artistic development, hoping for a strand of shared passion to bubble up from the collective interests of the class.

Why is it valuable to choose a central focus like this? I find it intensifies children's work and interests. It brings them together with a communal sense of learning and exploration. We still enjoy building, drawing, drama, playdough, and all the other activities in the classroom, but we will also begin to focus more on activities and conversations about "Tricks, Treasures, and the *Titanic*." Children's play is incorporating these ideas naturally, but I will also be bringing in new materials and provoking experiences that highlight these themes. For example, I've already begun to provision gemlike stones, beads, and coins, and collect resources about treasure, the *Titanic*, pirates, and more. And the children have proceeded to bury their treasure under every rock, log, fabric square, and carpet square they can find. All of these natural and unstructured materials are props we keep in the building area for children to incorporate in their constructive and dramatic play.

Why is it valuable to choose a theme that children are demonstrating an interest in? I find that children display a much higher level of energy and engagement for their work when it centers around subjects of their choosing. Though I will often bring in unrelated art activities, cooking projects, science experiments, and so on, I try to intersperse those with deep study around topics children are passionate about. In addition, I will try to extend that exploration for as long as possible, going deeper into certain areas or letting the children's questions lead us off on new tangents.

—SARAH, TEACHER

As the weeks and months progressed, Sarah used her observations to add more props and write more postings, telling the story of how her project ideas were progressing. Two examples are extracted below, in which she describes the connections that were being made with a project on homelessness in the room across the hall and her decision to have the children build treasure boxes.

Making Connections

Emily, Julia, and Zabia played a rather involved treasure game that seemed to reflect some of the ideas from the Uri Shulevitz story *The Treasure*, which we had read the day before. Interested in the ways they were revisiting and revising the story, I took pictures and recorded some of their words while they played.

I was particularly touched by the connection I saw to the work around collecting coins to give to homeless people that the Starlight class had been telling us about. I sensed the influence of that learning in their responses to the story about treasure. Shulevitz's story begins, "There once was a man and his name was Isaac. He lived in such poverty that again and again he went to bed hungry."

I am beginning to see a connection between the kind of treasure gathering, counting, and collecting these children are doing in the block area and the gathering of real coins they have undertaken as part of their exploration of homelessness issues.   —SARAH, TEACHER

Drawing and Designing Treasure Boxes

As a continuation of our Treasure project, I brought the children to our studio space in groups of three or four to work on designing and building treasure boxes. Each child first drew her ideas for a treasure box and told me her words about it. Then I provided some basic materials (cardboard, Popsicle sticks, masking tape, glue) for building their ideas. Some children referred to their drawings in making the transfer from two to three dimensions, while others just let the materials be their inspiration. There were lots of good opportunities for physical problem solving as children struggled with how to make walls stand up, how to stick things together, and how to form the shapes they desired. I asked a few encouraging questions like "Is there a space to put the treasure?" and "Will your box have a lid?" Mostly children experimented with their own materials and also watched each other for good ideas. Some children asked others for help with holding things up, tearing off pieces of tape, and so on. It was wonderful to see the collaboration that can occur when small groups of children work together in the focused, protected space of the studio.   —SARAH, TEACHER

Analyzing your documentation helps you find underlying themes and connections between what the children are saying and doing with one another. Publicly articulating your thinking process solicits input from your coworkers and the children's families. This is a powerful way to keep your curriculum planning creative, relevant, and on target.

When you see children involved in play or conversation over the course of several days or weeks, study your notes and photographs for possible underlying themes that can launch an in-depth curriculum project. Offer additional props to keep it going, along with descriptions and photos for the children to hear and see what you have noticed about their interest. Use their responses as input for what to do next. Post this as a story, along with photos and any transcripts of conversations, as Sarah Felstiner did.

Post Documentation of the Learning You Are Planning For

Most early childhood programs are required to post their curriculum plans. If you are using your observations to guide your planning, you should post your thinking about this. One option is to set up a bulletin board display with brief descriptions of the learning domains you are planning for. Under each description, put a clear plastic sleeve where you can insert written notes and photos of your observations of children's learning. You can find descriptions of the categories in any number of professional resources. You might want to use *Mind in the Making: The Seven Essential Life Skills Every Child Needs* by Ellen Galinsky or *The Portfolio and Its Use, Book II: A Road Map for Assessment* by Sharon MacDonald.

Consider creating your own learning outcome categories in simple, child-friendly language. Create a visual system for sorting and displaying your notes and photos. This will demonstrate that you are carefully watching and thinking about what is unfolding among the children in your room. This is really the intent behind requirements for teachers to display curriculum plans and do portfolio assessments. Each week, you can move your posted documentation into individual children's portfolios, making duplicate copies when more than one child is involved.

Use Your Observations for Assessment

In the early childhood field, writing up observations is usually approached as an assessment task or a requirement imposed by supervisors. This often leads to teachers viewing children within a particular focus or using a checklist. While there are valuable uses for this kind of data collection, the process and form it takes tends to have a clinical, rather than human, quality to it. More often than not, when the write-up leaves the teacher's hands, it ends up in a forgotten file or on the floor of a parent's car. The effort the teacher has made in these situations leaves no one particularly thoughtful or eager for more.

Assessing children can be significantly more authentic when you use your daily observations to inform the process. Early childhood programs increasingly have some assessment tool in place to demonstrate accountability to

school-readiness guidelines or state-adopted early learning frameworks. This might be any one of a number of commercially available tools or an assessment system you have developed on your own over the years. Many programs use a portfolio system with collections of children's work and documentation stories about the children's engagement and learning in the curriculum you offer.

Whether purchased or created on your own, it is important to anchor any system for tracking children's learning in an early learning framework that incorporates research—yours and that of the profession as a whole. Then, as you study your observations, you can turn to this framework to find relevant research that your observations provide an example of.

For instance, as you review your documentation, you can choose to reference *Mind in the Making* and track children's learning in the seven "essential life skills" Galinsky (2010) cites as key predictors of success in life. These include the following:

- focus and self-control
- perspective taking
- communicating
- making connections
- critical thinking
- taking on challenges
- self-directed, engaged learning

Here's an example of how to include a reference to *Mind in the Making* in writing an observation story.

Kendra—A Focused and Self-Directed Learner

Today Kendra spent nearly forty minutes working with the small paper cups that she discovered the teachers had set up as an invitation. Other children came and went, but Kendra stayed focused and determined to discover how to get the cups to balance as she wanted them to. Her initial approach didn't work, and after several collapses of the cups she was stacking, Kendra devised a new approach. She added several cups nested together on top of the bottom one. Adding the next cup was still tricky, but Kendra continued to concentrate and focus on getting it to balance. Once she perfected her strategy, she replicated it again and again. Seeing her teacher photographing the process, Kendra asked to borrow the camera, saying, "Need to show. Need to show."

Many things impressed us about Kendra's work with the cups. We can easily see how she is thinking not only like an architectural engineer but like a scientist testing out her theory and replicating it successfully. In this observation we can see many of the seven essential life skills the research in *Mind in the Making* (Galinsky 2010) suggests will make Kendra a successful lifelong learner. As I reviewed this observation, I found I could easily highlight Kendra demonstrating self-directed, engaged learning; focus and self-control; and the ability to take on challenges.

—LUZ AND MARGIE,
TEACHER COACHES

If you are required to complete a formal assessment such as *Teaching Strategies GOLD®*, studying your observations and photos will give you plenty of data to input into its thirty-eight learning objectives for readiness. Perhaps you work with other required assessment checklists. Your detailed notes and photographs can illustrate the desired progress for a more meaningful report than just the checklist itself. Compare the two options here, one from an assessment book and the other from the observation notes of Sarah Felstiner. Can you guess which one is likely to end up posted on the refrigerator and which on the floor of the family car?

MATH CONCEPTS CHECKLIST

- ☑ Sorts objects according to function, size, and shape.
- ☑ Identifies circle, square, triangle, rectangle.
- ☑ Exhibits an understanding of one-to-one correspondence.
- ☑ Duplicates sequential order of objects or pictures.
- ☑ Understands simple measurement techniques.

January 10

In the studio this morning, Emily and some friends were making masks. Emily offered to help Alex attach some string to hold the mask on. She cut a piece of string, but it was too short to reach around Alex's head. She said, "Maybe this can be for Maria's mask, this extra string, 'cause she has a little face."

Emily cut another piece, but it was too long. She said, "How 'bout we cut half of it off and try it again?"

Both of these comments show a sophisticated understanding of relationships between length, circumference, size, and other math concepts, as well as displaying Emily's thoughtfulness about her friends.

—SARAH, TEACHER

The more resourceful and knowledgeable you become about learning domain content, the more you can insert information from professional resources right into your documentation stories. Notice how toddler teacher Darlene Nantarath does this in the following story.

Exploring Lines

Sophia, not quite two years old, sat down with a basket of Kapla blocks (think rectangles). We started together by stacking the pieces on top of each other, making them taller and taller. Then when the pile fell over, Sophia used each of the pieces, one by one, to line them up side by side, forming parallel lines. Then her work took a different path when she started taking one piece at a time and connecting each end together, making a long line. What made her switch from stacking to parallel lines to connecting each end? Did she see the pieces differently every time she used her hands to move them around?

Sophia is exploring different ways of using her materials and learning relationships between space, size, and shapes. The materials and the way she is exploring them are helping her understand the lines and become a constructive and creative thinker.

How do lines benefit a child's development? Through this experience, Sophia is gaining more understanding of how lines can connect together and the relationships between them (distance, space, on top of, shapes, and so on). Working with lines will support Sophia's later development of constructing letters, patterns, and geometric shapes.

"Identifying and following vertical, horizontal, diagonal, and other kinds of lines helps children see and understand how shapes, letters, patterns, and buildings are constructed—and helps them to form their own constructions" (Topal 2005).

—DARLENE, TEACHER

Darlene increasingly uses addendums to her documentation stories that include professional descriptions on the stages of learning for different domains. Here's an example of one she uses with observations of block play.

Why Is Block Play Important?

Block play provides an open outlet for children to express themselves and acts as a way for them to build upon what they see and what they understand of certain concepts in their world. They use blocks to symbolically represent objects and concepts in their own world. By observing children in block play and analyzing their constructions, adults gain insight into how the children perceive the world around them. In addition to helping adults understand children's theories, blocks play an important role in the early development stages, especially from the toddler to preschool stage. Blocks are open-ended materials that promote self-directed play.

Adults could easily overlook block play as a valuable stage in early childhood. Blocks are unique materials that continue to expand children's ideas and creativity. As an educator, I have observed the different stages of block play, asked questions, and reviewed with other educators how the children are using the materials and what may happen next.

Stages of Block Play:

- **Stage I: Carrying.** Children carry blocks around, but they are not used for construction. Children typically gather blocks and dump them. This is the beginning of children exploring concepts such as *more, less, thin, thick, large,* and *small.* This helps young toddlers refine their fine- and gross-motor skills.

- **Stage II: Building Begins.** Mostly making rows, either horizontal (on the floor) or vertical (stacked). There is much repetition in this early building pattern, which is basically functional play with blocks. Over time they take more risks, and their stacks and towers become more imaginative.

- **Stage III: Bridging.** Children's structures begin to have two blocks with a space between them, spanned or connected by a third block. During this phase, children use their problem-solving skills as they explore spatial relationships. They examine ways to support two blocks and join them together with a third block.

- **Stage IV: Enclosures.** Blocks are placed in such a way that they are enclosing a space. Bridging and enclosures are among the earliest technical problems children have to solve when playing with blocks, and they occur soon after a child begins to use blocks regularly. Children repeat and refine the process as they experiment with joined enclosures and consider how the varying shapes and sizes of blocks impact their enclosures.

- **Stage V: Becoming More Imaginative in Their Block Building.** They use more blocks and create more elaborate designs, incorporating patterns and balance into their constructions. Children express competencies with block building and now take risks and express more imaginative attributes, including defined symmetry, in their construction. They discover how spatial relationships impact building.

- **Stage VI: Naming of Structures for Dramatic Play Beings.** Before this stage, children may have named their structures, but not necessarily based on the function of the building. This stage of block building corresponds to the "realistic" stage in art development. These structures are complex, with bridges, enclosures, towers, and complicated designs.

- **Stage VII: Resembling or Naming for Play.** Children reproduce and construct structures based on their daily life experiences. The names of the structures correspond with the intended function of the structure. Children may express what they intend to build prior to acquiring the blocks to start construction. (Wardle 2002, 243–44)

—Darlene Nantarath, October 2011

Consider the New Zealand Learning Story Approach

Early childhood educators in Aotearoa, New Zealand, have developed a particular approach to writing observations stories. Professor Margaret Carr and her New Zealand colleagues created the Learning Story approach not only as a way to assess desirable outcomes for children but as a means to strengthen teachers' ability to use documentation as a tool for their own learning and teaching. An interesting feature of how many New Zealand educators use Learning Stories is to write them directly to the child, which some people have characterized as akin to a love letter. This brings your voice as an educator into the story powerfully, always conveying a sense of how competent the children are. Building on the initial conventions developed in New Zealand, our U.S. colleague, Tom Drummond, suggests working with the following guidelines for becoming familiar with writing a Learning Story.

1   **What happened:** Begin with descriptive details about what the children are saying and doing, adding reflections on your own interest in what you see them exploring. Write with the voice of someone who cares deeply and is listening closely to discover what is happening. You are curious. You have a strong image of the child.

2   **What you think it means:** Write about what you see as the significance of this observation. This meaning-making is best done in a dialogue with other teachers and the children's families. You consider such things as culture, context, and child development theories. Perhaps you can connect the observation with other things you know about this child from past experience. You can also include reference here to early learning standards and desired outcomes.

3   **Opportunities and possibilities:** Write about what you are thinking as possibilities for doing next and why. Include any curiosity, hypotheses, or questions that are on your mind as you describe your choices of how to respond. This gives the reader insight into how teachers think about what they do.

4   **Invite the family's perspective:** Pose a question or two as an invitation for the family to respond, expressing your eagerness to hear their perspective on this Learning Story.

5   **Give the story a title:** Like every good story, your Learning Story should have a title, one that synthesizes what you see as most significant to make visible.

Now that you know the conventions for the New Zealand approach to writing Learning Stories, you will recognize that several of the sample observation displays at the end of each study session in chapters 4–11 have adopted this approach. The following is another example. As you read Miss Simone's Learning Story, notice how she has captured each of the key elements of the New Zealand Learning Story conventions.

"It's a Tower!"

October 20

Dear Anders,

Since you've joined our school, teachers have noticed how much you enjoy exploring your environment and figuring out how things work. You seem fascinated with concepts of gravity, trajectory, and cause-and-effect relationships. Over time we've observed your discovery of inclined planes, pulleys, water wheels, cranks, and levers. Something that has impressed me in particular is your inclination to build symmetrical block structures. Since April I have witnessed you building and rebuilding the same structure, adding new aspects as you become more comfortable with the materials and gain confidence in your balancing and building skills. I've also noticed that you remember and learn from the challenges you encounter when building with blocks. The very first time you built your structure, you attempted building it very tall, very fast, and a block accidentally fell on your toes. Ouch!

When you built your structure again this week, it was clear you had learned how to avoid that mishap:

Miss Simone: "What are you building?"

Anders: "It's a tower! This is good, and I'm almost all done."

Miss Simone: "It seems like you have a plan, Anders. What happens next?"

Anders: "Nothing else. When it goes up to the sky, it falls down because it's too tall. So I don't want to do it."

Miss Simone: "Would you like some help making your tower taller?"

Anders: "I'm not gonna add anything else, because I don't want it to drop on me. So I'm all done now!"

Anders, I am excited to see that through *exploration* and *experimentation* with materials, you are developing *working theories* for making sense of the world around you. You are beginning to understand the nature and *properties* of objects and substances in the environment. You are learning how to manipulate these objects as a *creative outlet* and a tool for *self-expression*. You are also learning *strategies* for active *thinking* and *reasoning* by *reflecting* on your experiences and *solving problems* you encounter along the way. This is an important cognitive skill and developmental milestone for a three-year-old.

I wonder whether you would like to teach a friend how to build a tower. You could make a how-to book to share with others: you could take pictures of your structure, and I'd help you write down your words. Have you thought of incorporating other materials into your building process? We have cardboard tubes, plastic spools, fabric, and Plexiglas sheets available in the block room to help you extend and expand your plans and ideas. I wonder what the next version of your tower might look like.

Anders, I feel privileged to be able to witness your *learning journey* here at Crescent Park and look forward to seeing what other discoveries and connections you will make during your time with us!

Fondly,

MISS SIMONE

Make Your Vision for Childhood Visible

As you become a more observant, aware teacher, your teaching practice will be transformed. You will find more satisfying relationships with the children and their families. Your curriculum and learning outcomes will be more significant and authentic. Developing the art of mindfulness tends to bring more pleasure and liveliness to your overall life. You'll start noticing all kinds of details that keep your senses active and your heart humming. This inspires others, who will begin to sit up and take notice. Who is this lively person, and what makes her or him so enjoyable and interesting to be around? As a result of your influence, others will begin to see children as a source of enrichment for their lives. They will see you as a model for the kind of life they'd like to be living. In effect, you become a leader, someone who is able to help others discover new potential in themselves.

As you bring your image of children and your vision for childhood alive, assuming leadership will be a natural result of developing the art and skill of awareness. Once you are on the road, casting a light ahead, others will want to join in and help shape the path. Look back at the poem in two voices that started this book. The tug-of-war that teachers find in themselves can be diffused by becoming careful listeners, observers, and narrators. The stories we gather and make visible can reassure parents and supervisors and make teaching a more satisfying and compelling profession. Joining our voices two by two, we can become a persuasive chorus, bringing our communities more in tune with the value of childhood.

References

Carson, Rachel. 1998. *The Sense of Wonder*. New York: HarperCollins.

Dillard, Annie. 1993. *The Living*. New York: Harper Perennial.

Elkind, David. 2007. *The Hurried Child: Growing Up Too Fast Too Soon*, 3rd ed. Cambridge, MA: Da Capo Press.

Forman, George. 1999. REGGIO-L@vmd.cso.uiuc.edu.

Galinksy, Ellen. 2010. *Mind in the Making: The Seven Essential Life Skills Every Child Needs*. New York: William Morrow Paperbacks.

Gallas, Karen. 1994. *The Languages of Learning: How Children Talk, Write, Dance, Draw, and Sing Their Understanding of the World*. New York: Teachers College Press.

Gopnik, Alison. 2010. *The Philosophical Baby: What Children's Minds Tell Us about Truth, Love, and the Meaning of Life*. New York: Picador.

Hoffman, Donald D. 2000. *Visual Intelligence: How We Create What We See*. New York: W. W. Norton & Company.

Hoffman, Eric. 2004. *Magic Capes, Amazing Powers: Transforming Superhero Play in the Classroom*. St. Paul, MN: Redleaf Press.

Kent, Corita, and Jan Steward. 2008. *Learning by Heart: Teaching to Free the Spirit*. New York: Allsworth Press.

Pelo, Ann, and Fran Davidson. 2000. *That's Not Fair! A Teacher's Guide to Activism with Young Children*. St. Paul, MN: Redleaf Press.

Rico, Gabriele. 2000. *Writing the Natural Way*. New York: Tarcher.

Schafer, William M. 2004. "The Infant as Reflection of Soul: The Time before There Was a Self." *Zero to Three* 24 (3): 4–8.

Topal, Cathy Weisman. 2005. *Thinking with a Line Teacher's Guide*. Worcester, MA: Davis Publications.

Wardle, Francis. 2002. *Introduction to Early Childhood Education: A Multidimensional Approach to Child-Centered Care and Learning*. Boston, MA: Allyn & Bacon.

Additional Resources

Abbott, Shirley. 1998. *Womenfolks: Growing Up Down South*. Boston: Houghton Mifflin Company.

Andrews, Valerie. 1990. *A Passion for This Earth: Exploring a New Partnership of Man, Woman, and Nature*. New York: HarperCollins.

Bruchac, Joseph. 1997. *Tell Me a Tale: A Book about Storytelling*. San Diego: Harcourt Children's

Carr, Margaret. 2001. *Assessment in Early Childhood Settings: Learning Stories*. Thousand Oaks, CA: Sage Publications.

Carr, Margaret, and Wendy Lee. 2012. *Learning Stories: Constructing Learner Identities in Early Education*. Thousand Oaks, CA: SAGE Publications.

Chard, Sylvia C., and Yvonne Kogan. 2009. *From My Side: Being a Child*. Lewisville, NC: Gryphon House.

Delpit, Lisa. 2006. *Other People's Children: Cultural Conflict in the Classroom*. New York: The New Press.

Felsteiner, Sarah. 1999. "Show and Tell: Documenting Young Children's Emergent Curriculum." Unpublished Masters Thesis

Gopnik, Allison, Andrew N. Meltzoff, and Patricia K. Kuhl. 2000. *The Scientist in the Crib: What Early Learning Tells Us about the Mind*. New York: William Morrow Paperbacks.

Keller, Helen. 2012. *The World I Live In*. Los Angeles: Indo-European Publishing.

Kohl, Herbert R. 1996. *Should We Burn Babar? Essays on Children's Literature and the Power of Stories*. New York: The New Press.

Louv, Richard. 2005. *Last Child in the Woods: Saving Our Children from Nature-Deficit Disorder*. Chapel Hill, NC: Algonquin Books.

———. 2011. *The Nature Principle: Human Restoration and the End of Nature-Deficit Disorder*. Chapel Hill, NC: Algonquin Books.

MacDonald, Sharon. 1997. *The Portfolio and Its Use, Book II: A Road Map for Assessment*. Little Rock, AR: Southern Early Childhood Association.

Mason, Jerry. 1977. *The Family of Children*. New York: Putnam Publishing Group.

N.E.Thing Enterprises. 1993. *Magic Eye: A New Way of Looking at the World*. Kansas City, MO: N.E. Thing Enterprises.

Pelo, Ann. 2007. *The Language of Art: Inquiry-Based Studio Practices in Early Childhood Settings*. St. Paul, MN: Redleaf Press.

Reynolds, Gretchen, and Elizabeth Jones. 1997. *Master Players: Learning from Children at Play*. New York: Teachers College Press.

Ruef, Kerry. 2012. The Private Eye:"5X"Looking/Thinking by Analogy—A Guide to Developing the Interdisciplinary Mind. http://www.the-private-eye.com/index.html.

Smith, Robert Paul. 2010. *Where Did You Go? Out. What Did You Do? Nothing*. New York: W. A. Norton and Company

Whitman, Walt. 2008. *Leaves of Grass*. Produced by G. Fuhrman and David Widger. Project Gutenberg. http://www.gutenberg.org/files/1322/1322-h/1322-h.htm#2H_4_0193.

Wilks, Mike. 1997. *Metamorphosis: The Ultimate Spot-the-Difference Book*. New York: Penguin.

Wood, A. J. 1992. *Look: The Ultimate Spot-the-Difference Book*. New York: Puffin Pied Piper.

Index